Peter on Leadership: A Contemporary Exegetical Analysis

Steven Crowther

Copyright © 2012 Steven Crowther

All rights reserved.

ISBN:9780615747255
ISBN-13:0615747256

DEDICATION

This book is dedicated to my loving, dedicated and amazing wife, Terri. She has helped me over the many years of marriage as a partner together in life, in ministry, in suffering, and in joy. She has taught me how to live in faith and optimism, yet live in touch with the realities of life. I would not have made it in ministry or academic endeavors without her constant encouragement, insight, and steadfastness, as well as her real, demonstrated love.

CONTENTS

	Acknowledgments	i
1	Leadership and Theology	3
2	Models and Questions for Leadership	10
3	Socio-Rhetorical Examination and Interpretation	18
4	Preliminary Research in Peter	23
5	Preliminary Research in Paul's Writings (Philippians 2:5-11)	35
6	The Contemporary Context of Leadership	44
7	The Exegetical Process	51
8	The Text of 1 Peter	65
9	1 Peter – Pericope 1	68
10	1 Peter – Pericope 2	80
11	1 Peter – Pericope 3	98
12	1 Peter – Pericope 4	110
13	1 Peter – Pericope 5	120
14	1 Peter – The Big Picture	139
15	Principles from Peter	147
16	Peter in Contemporary Context	156
17	Peter in the Context of Paul	160
18	Peter in the Context of the Church	167
19	Peter in the Context of Contemporary Business	173
20	Conclusion – Ancient Wisdom in Context	181
	References	184

Steven Crowther

ACKNOWLEDGMENTS

The completion of this endeavor would not have been possible without the help of many others around me. First and foremost, I would like to aknowledge the Lord Jesus Christ who changed my life and made this possible because of His work in my life. The Lord has helped me throughout life to continue to pursue more understanding of Him and His ways through many methods, including academic endeavors such as this one represented in this book. He has given me gifts to help me in these endeavors and a passion to pursue them. The Lord is not only the source, but also the object of this study in learning leadership from Him and His way of leadership. This study would not have been possible without the subjective work of the Lord in my life and the objective work of the Lord in and through the Scriptures.

I am deeply grateful to Dr. Corne Bekker, my mentor though this process. His insights and counsel during this learning process were both valuable and helpful, not only in this academic process, but also in the process of life and ministry. Dr. Bekker expressed genuine care and concern, as well as academic and spirtual insight during this process of my spiritual and academic growth. He helped me to see the hand of God in the process several times when I needed insight. I am deeply grateful for this personal connection that facilitated growth in so many ways in my life and my understanding of life and ministry.

In addition, I would like to acknowledge Dr. Bruce Winston as the Dean of the School of Global Leadership and Entrepreneurship of Regent University, as well as the faculty and staff. They were not only kind and helpful, they were also encouraging in many ways and on several different levels, from administrative to academic areas. Clearly, I have been changed in positive ways by this process at Regent University, in areas of understanding, academics, pedagogy, and spirituality. Most of this postive change came through a combination of interactions with faculty and administrators at this school, as well as through the process that has developed at this school. I would also like to acknowledge Dr. Doris Gomez and Dr. Kathleen Patterson for their grace and encouragement in this writing process.

This process would not been as effective without the help and insights of my fellow students in the Global Leadership Cohort of 2008. Each of these students rallied around at important times to give encouragement, help, and hope in the process of our common academic studies. A special thanks to Nick Ertel for the cover design and graphics.

It is striking to see how twentieth-century scholars have all but ignored the topic of religious leadership.
    Michael J. McClymond

CHAPTER 1

LEADERSHIP AND THEOLOGY

Though leadership has been an issue of discussion for many centuries, as well as among recent researchers, there has been little agreement on the description of leadership. The philosopher Plato, Machiavelli, and James Madison wrote specifically on the issue of leadership (Guinness, 2000). In the 20th century, leadership has been a topic of study by researchers with no consensus on the definition of leadership, only that it concerns influence in the accomplishment of group objectives (House, Hanges, Javidian, Dorfman, & Gupta, 2004). This vast array of differing conceptions of leadership has created a bewildering body of literature with differences from one writer to another in the field of leadership (Yukl, 2002). However, in the midst of this discussion, has entered the concept of spirituality and its effect on leadership. Weber (1968) based his concepts for religious leadership upon the lives of certain religious leaders like Moses, Buddha, Mohammed, and Jesus. Nevertheless, McClymond (2001) found it striking that there was not much discussion of religious leadership among scholars in the 20th century. Yet, with the turn of the 21st century, there has been a turn to spirituality in leadership studies (Bekker, 2008). This turn to spirituality has included development of theories of leadership with a spiritual component like spiritual leadership (Frye, 2003), servant leadership (Patterson, 2003), and authentic leadership (Avolio, Gardner, Walumbwa, & May, 2004; Klenke, 2007). This turn to spirituality in leadership studies has also included distinctively Christian leadership models like kenotic leadership (Bekker, 2006). However, these were not the first to discuss leadership in the context of Christianity. Authors who discussed leadership in the context of the teachings of Christianity have included Augustine, Martin Luther, and the writers of the Christian Scriptures (Guinness, 2000). Some of the writers of Christian

Scriptures who addressed leadership were Mark, Paul, and Peter. Research has been done by some authors on the impact of the writers of Christian Scripture and the ministry of Jesus (Bekker, 2006; Self, 2009; Zarate, 2009) on contemporary leadership. Clinton (1988) developed leadership emergence theory based upon his broad study of leaders in the Hebrew and Christian Scriptures.

Nevertheless, this source for leadership theory needs further investigation for at least two reasons. First, this is a new area of research for contemporary leadership that has only gained ascendancy since the turn of the century. Second, this is a broad source for research in the area of leadership and much more needs to be done to develop profundity as well as breadth from this rich resource.

In response to this need, some scholarly journals have begun in the 21st century, such as *The Journal for Biblical Perspectives in Leadership* and *The Journal of Religious Leadership*, to promote research in the areas of Christian Scriptures, spirituality, and leadership. In this area of research, there is much to be examined and gained for contemporary leadership development and understanding. In contemporary leadership, one result of neglecting the spiritual dimension in leadership is a void of values and, in response to many public failures, a movement of spirituality is awakening in businesses across the country (Gibbons, 2008). In the context of this nexus of Christian spirituality and leadership possibly there is a way to discover new models for effective leadership for the future. Many contemporary theories of leadership have focused primarily on behavior like leadership practices (Kouzes & Posner, 2007), transformational leadership, and the skills or style approach (Northouse, 2004); while others focused on the culture of the organization (Cameron & Quinn, 2006) including an emphasis on changing leadership behavior.

Yet, leadership is not just behaviors or styles; it involves internal issues as well. Character is central to good leadership and character is the inner form that makes a person who he or she is and it provides the leader's deepest source of bearings (Guinness, 2000). The issue of personhood or ontology comes to the fore in this discussion and involves spirituality particularly as found in the Christian Scriptures. This is an issue that is addressed by

Jesus, Paul, and Peter in the Christian Scriptures of not only behavior but personhood, or the being of the leader—the ontology of the leader. Though those like Machiavelli (1515/1908) said that internal issues such as character and integrity are not important components of leadership, writers of the Christian Scriptures disagree. In 1 Peter, Peter exhorted the leaders to follow the example of Jesus in leading like a shepherd and the main point is the way this leadership is exercised along with character description of what it takes to be a leader (Witherington, 2007). The exhortation found in 1 Peter to leaders is short, but based upon issues of ontology as found in earlier sections of 1 Peter. Therefore, the writing of 1 Peter needs thorough examination for understanding teaching concerning leadership and its proper appropriation for contemporary contexts.

Leadership studies do not generally embrace theology in the process of research nor is there usually a convergence of theology and leadership (Ayers, 2006). However, in the past, theology or research from the Christian Scriptures has been a valuable source of research. Medieval theologians believed that theology was the queen of the sciences (that is, of the domains of knowledge) and philosophy was her handmaid; but in our day, theology has been largely banished from the university (DeWeese & Moreland, 2005). However, theology has fallen from this place of prominence to be replaced by pragmatism and empiricism. Instead of searching for truth in theological foundations, truth is now sought in answering questions of function. Does it work in accomplishing the objectives? If something accomplishes certain determined objectives then it is assumed that it is true and truth can be found for developing a theory. Nevertheless, this is quite Aristotelian that truth lies in the physical world. It would be more productive to find truth then apply it to the physical world; a move from internals to externals. While this sounds Platonic, it is not Platonic thinking that drives this as much as theological thinking. Thinking theologically is a view from the perspective of divine intention and prerogative rather than a view from below which is anthropological—an effort to find truth as it happens—and is troubled by misshapen self-issues. Many times science asks for an outside objective viewpoint, but is that possible when we study ourselves and we are the researcher and the researched?

Theology lifts us out of this research circle so we can catch a glimpse from above concerning the human issue of leadership. Nevertheless, theology is not unacquainted with the necessity of circularity since no quest for truth can escape from the necessity of this hermeneutic circle, linking the encounter with reality to an interpretive point of view, so science and theology are joined in a relationship of mutual illumination and correction (Polkinghorne, 2007). Theology must be brought back to the research arena, not to displace science, but as a partner in a search for truth that is more than empirical. In the context of the 21st century and this turn to spirituality in leadership studies, this provides a rich new resource for leadership in the Christian Scriptures and the theology from places such as 1 Peter. Science and theology are both concerned with the search for truth and they share common ways of approaching this search for understanding as well as sharing a common conviction that there is truth to be sought (Polkinghorne, 2007). Therefore, it is in this convergence of science or research and theology that truth is sought for leadership in the contemporary setting.

The Problem in Leadership

The world is in desperate need of a different leadership model, with corporate leaders taking advantage of their position, leaders of undeveloped countries producing more poverty, and church leaders compromising their churches through lack of integrity (Blanchard & Hodges, 2005). The present leadership crisis affects all segments of society. Even leadership in the church borrows models of leadership from the business world (Guinness, 1993; McGrath, 2002), the latest corporate scandals have awakened our corporate conscious to the fact that self-interest unchecked by moral reasoning and obligation results in destructive greed. Because leaders wield such power in society, this calls for an examination of moral underpinnings and the moral status of leaders in society (Gardner & Avolio, 2005). This call for an examination is a serious issue for leadership studies. Though leadership studies have produced some profound insights, this research has not found a foundation upon which to build a consistently effective model of leadership that includes ontological as well as cultural and behavioral issues. Most leadership theories are focused on processes at only one level because it is difficult to develop a multilevel theory that is parsimonious and applicable (Yukl, 2002). This difficulty has promoted leadership theories and models with limited success.

Leadership is a phenomenon that has intrigued humans since people began organizing. The concept of organizations is now moving away from mechanistic creations that once flourished to relational aspects that can be compared to changes in understanding the universe as relational and changing rather than static; from Newtonian physics to quantum physics (Wheatley, 1999). New sciences have developed new discoveries not only in the physical universe but have challenged social realities like leadership. These new ways of thinking have provided insights for leadership theory but have not solved the issues of consistent effective leadership.

In addition to science, history can provide insights for leadership theory and models. It is presumptuous to act as if leadership philosophy was born in the 20th century; leadership theory is firmly grounded in the archives of history (Galbraith & Galbraith, 2004). History involves both changes from one era to another as well as continuity through time. This tension in human life, as examined in the context of history, can both inform us and render service to human life (Breisach, 2007). This service includes understanding of leadership and its effectiveness in the contexts of different settings. The examination of 1 Peter not only involves theology, it involves history as lived out in the context of the church in the 1st century. This has value that is theological and historical, as well as practical. Human life is never lived in the present alone but in three worlds—one that is, one that was, and one that will be—and we experience them as inextricably linked and influencing each other (Breisach, 2007). This influence includes influence upon leadership theory and models. The problem is that much research in the area of leadership looks to the present for answers that can only be found in the context of history—past, present, and future.

The ultimate point of studying leadership is to answer the question of good leadership in two senses—effective and morally good—but the problem with existing leadership research is that few studies investigate both senses of good leadership and when they do, they do not fully explore the moral implications of their research (Ciulla, 2004). Study of leadership that is theologically driven from the Christian Scriptures can explore these two senses and the underlying assumption is that they are connected; therefore the connection is implicit in the material that is researched and will find its way into the leadership concepts.

The problem is twofold. The first aspect of the problem is that there is a crisis of leadership in contemporary society that is at least partially due to internal issues of leadership, such as character, that is rarely addressed in the research. The recent headlines have sharpened the outcry for a new standard of integrity in leadership with higher standards of character (Gardner & Avolio, 2005). The second aspect of the problem is that the source of leadership studies often propagates this weakness. Many studies examine what is effective in leadership by examining the behaviors of effective leaders (Fiedler, 1967; House, 1971; Kouzes & Pozner, 2007). However, this does not address the internal issues of character and ontology. The problem, therefore, is not only a crisis in leadership but also a certain circular reasoning in finding a way out by examining leaders as they exist.

Many churches do not have a clear understanding of Christian leadership because they have drawn their understanding of leadership from their successful members who have been trained in secular systems, and since the church leaders function from this platform, these leaders cannot help those in their congregation to lead biblically (Zarate, 2009). The church continues this dilemma by examining leaders as they exist particularly in the business world. Pastors and business leaders were found to be strikingly similar when comparing interview narratives with business leadership literature, including their underlying values and leadership practices (Zook, 1993). The pressure to succeed in bringing more people into the church has led to the adoption of a business style approach with a business model in the church (McGrath, 2002). The problem of leadership exists in the church in its imitation of the models that have been developed empirically rather than biblically.

The way ahead could be to find a new source such as that which is found in the Christian Scriptures, not as an adjunct to research, but as the source—as the Queen of the Sciences. General studies of principles from the broad context of Scripture have value, but in searching for a leadership solution in the midst of crisis two things are needed. One is a depth that can be found in specific studies in the Scriptures such as that found in Peter and his leadership, as well as his exhortations to leaders. Two, is a situation in which leaders found themselves in crisis in history, but in a similar way to the contemporary context. The leaders in Peter's fraternity were in double crises that of pressure to lead like the society around them and the fact that they were living in the midst of persecution for their faith. It was in this context that Peter both led as an example of leadership and exhorted his co-leaders.

Despite the abundance of writing on the topic, leadership has presented a major challenge to practitioners and researchers interested in understanding the nature of leadership.
  Peter G. Northouse

CHAPTER 2

MODELS AND QUESTIONS FOR LEADERSHIP

This study explored the leadership principles as found in 1 Peter and the example of Peter as a leader. This research examined these principles of leadership in application to contemporary leadership while comparing them to two contemporary models of leadership, authentic leadership and kenotic leadership. These two theories have identified internal issues of spirituality as needed components of contemporary leadership. One of the theories, kenotic leadership is founded upon principles from another author of the Christian Scriptures, the Apostle Paul. This theory was developed from research in Philippians 2.

Therefore, the purpose of this study was to discover principles for leadership from a specific theological base found in the writings of Peter and compare it to another theory with a theological base as found in the writings of Paul. Further, the purpose was to compare the principles as found in the writings of Peter with a contemporary theory that included spirituality and internal issues of integrity as found in authentic leadership. Can this theological approach from the writings of Peter inform or challenge contemporary theological models and bring insight for the present crisis of leadership?

Theological studies have recently been relegated to divinity studies with use only in the development of doctrine. However, since this turn to spirituality has occurred, there has been some research based in theology for contemporary leadership (Bekker, 2006; Clinton, 1988, Niewold, 2006; Winston, 2002, Zarate, 2009). While some have been an examination of specific scriptures in examining leadership concepts, none have examined the writings of Peter in this pursuit. In addition, these examinations have compared their findings with other contemporary theories but none have been compared with authentic leadership or with a theory of leadership that is founded upon Scripture as well but from another biblical author.

Authentic leadership is a model wherein leaders are true to their core values and have a profound sense of purpose that they are aware of themselves and others perceive this awareness, as well as aware of their context while being hopeful, confident, and high in moral character (Gardner & Avolio, 2005). These genuine leaders lead from the perspective of knowing who they are and being open and transparent with their followers. In authentic leadership, the focus on transparency, positivity, and high ethical standards is critical (Avolio et al., 2004). According to Gardner and Avolio, authentic leaders are leaders who (a) know who they are and what they believe in, (b) are transparent in their values and actions, (c) focus on developing positive psychological states such as confidence, and (d) are known for their integrity. This combination of integrity and developing positive psychological states creates positive influence. Authentic leaders influence followers from a moral perspective. They create meaning and positively construct reality for themselves and their followers (Gardner & Avolio, 2005). This leadership model includes ontological issues on at least two levels. One, is the leader operates from a sense of who they are as a person from their being. Two, the leader constructs and defines reality showing the nature of what is real and how it applies to purpose. However, there is also a spiritual component. Spirituality and spiritual identity are at the core of authentic leadership (Klenke, 2007). Authentic leadership is ontological as well as spiritual with a high sense of morality.

Kenotic leadership is a model founded upon a pericope of Christian Scripture, Philippians 2:5-11, written by Paul. This model, developed in the 21st century, examines this portion of Scripture which is an exhortation to follow Jesus Christ and imitate His way of leadership. This theory proposes a mimetic Christological model of leadership (Bekker, 2007b). This concept is based on the kenosis or the relinquishment of privilege by Christ in His earthly ministry. This model encourages imitation of Christ in *kenosis* or self-emptying, servant posturing, embracing humanity, humility, and obedience in leading others (Bekker, 2007b). Kenosis is a divestment of power by the leader that allows for a new union that is marked by equality and service between leader and follower (Bekker, 2009). This model based in Philippians, which is established on the abasement, humility, and obedience of Christ, offers an alternative view of leadership that is oriented toward serving rooted in humility and common mutuality (Bekker, 2009). This kenosis speaks of the humility of Christ in taking the form of a servant by emptying Himself, but not laying aside His being of divinity (Berkhof, 1996). Through this process, Christ was exalted as leader of the entire human race. Here Paul provided the ultimate leadership model of Christ who set the perfect example for leadership which was a humble virtue-based model that everyone could embrace (Danley, 2009). Kenotic leadership is based upon the Scriptures with an exhortation to imitate Christ in His way of leadership.

In summary, the purpose of this study was to examine the instructions from 1 Peter concerning leadership which includes following the example of Christ. Further, the purpose was to explore this issue from a scholarly perspective that was exegetical in combination with research that was scientific. This exploration was then compared to contemporary leadership and to a leadership model derived from exegetical research in a different pericope of the Christian Scriptures.

The Relevant Question

Research questions are specific questions to be answered that further focus the purpose of the study (Creswell, 2009). The question for examination in this study was the following: What leadership style and practices were developed by Peter, particularly in 1 Peter, and do these practices and style support or negate the contemporary models of leadership in authentic or kenotic leadership? This question was answered through research using socio-rhetorical interpretation and its application in the book of 1 Peter in the Scriptures. This approach invited detailed attention to the text itself while moving interactively into the world of the people who wrote the texts and into our present world (Robbins, 1996). This close examination of the text of 1 Peter can provide answers for the initial issue of leadership issues found in this pericope which can then be compared to the other models found in contemporary leadership theory.

Why is This Important

The value of this study was that it has significance on several levels. On one level, this exploratory study examined leadership principles as found in the writings of Peter, specifically 1 Peter, in connection to contemporary leadership issues and theory. Of course, 1 Peter has been mined by others for theological and ecclesial issues (Davids, 1990; Green, 2007; Grudem, 1999; Jobes, 2005; Luther, 1990; Marshall, 1991; Witherington, 2007), but not in the context of leadership theory. A proper approach to the Christian Scriptures is to seek to submit to the text presuming the presence of communicative intent mediated through the text with a disciplined hearing of what the text is saying while being opened to a continuous process of listening and hearing (Hart, 2000).This exegetical analysis examined this section of the Christian Scriptures deeply, opened to the process of listening and hearing, to find and parse out insights for leadership concepts that are relevant to contemporary issues. The key to good biblical interpretation is to learn to read the text carefully and ask the right questions of the text and then seek the contemporary relevance of the text (Fee & Stuart, 1993). The questions of leadership were sought in the text while pursuing relevance for contemporary theories and models of leadership.

On another level, once these concepts were discovered and explained, they were compared and contrasted with both a contemporary theory of leadership that was based in sociological research as well as a contemporary theory that was based in exegetical analysis from a different portion of the Christian Scriptures. Authentic leadership, which contains a spiritual component, was compared to the concepts developed from Peter's life and writings about leadership in the context of spirituality. Did these two constructs provide insights for further depth in authentic leadership to provide a further theoretical foundation for the model or did they challenge the existing model of authentic leadership? This is important for this theory of leadership which is relatively new on the leadership research scene.

Uniquely, this study examined two portions of Christian Scripture to find their similarities or distinctions for leadership. This is an important issue. Did Paul and Peter teach two different ways of doing leadership; were they the same or could they build upon each other? This has ramifications for modern leadership research but it also has ramifications for the church. Significantly, this study examined leadership from the perspective of Peter while a majority of studies focus on the writings of Paul, specifically in the area of leadership and the Christian Scriptures. Witherington (2007), in his bibliography of 1 Peter, listed over 20 commentaries, with several studies on Peter and over 20 monographs, but none specifically on leadership; while a simple internet search yields over 150 books on leadership and the Apostle Paul. Attention to the gospels and the writings of Paul has tended to dominate the scholarly scene and these studies have left 1 Peter in a kind of canonical "twilight zone" where it is treated as an exegetical stepchild (Elliot, 2007). Therefore, it was imperative to bring the status of this text back to its historically recognized place of fully part of the cannon of Scripture. In addition, this research is significant in that over one billion people in the Roman Catholic Church look to Peter as the precedent or the model for leadership. First Peter is important because of its association with Peter in the early church attesting to the prominent role of Peter in the organization and history of the ancient church (Elliot, 2007). The Christian Scriptures mention Peter over 188 times and there can be no question that he is the most well-known of all of the original disciples of Jesus and, other than Jesus Himself, the humans that most shaped early Christianity were the two apostles, Peter and Paul (Witherington, 2007). According to traditional Catholic belief, the papacy was established by Jesus when he conferred its responsibilities and powers upon the apostle Peter at Caesarea Philippi and this exercise of the papacy or the Petrine ministry as exercised by the Bishop of Rome is recognized by the Catholic Church accepting him as the head of the worldwide earthly church (Mcbrien, 2000). The role of Peter was prominent in the early church and this role continues today in a large portion of the contemporary church. In spite of this, there has not been a great amount of specific research on Peter and leadership.

On yet another level, this research has implications for organizational leadership generally but also leadership in the church. The church has generally followed leadership models generated in the business world and have used the same measures for success (McGrath, 2002). Is this the best model for ecclesial leadership or is there another way ahead for the church? These

Christian Scriptures helped to form the church. In this formulation, is there counsel for leadership that is profound, relevant, and applicable to contemporary leadership issues? If this is so, this is very significant for the church and for leadership theory itself.

Finally, this study is significant in its use of socio-rhetorical interpretation in the examination of this portion of the Christian Scriptures. Socio-rhetorical interpretation approaches the text as though it were a thickly textured tapestry, in that, the text contains complex patterns and images and when looked at one way brings limited insight, but when looked at in multiple ways multiple textures and insights come into view (Robbins, 1996). This method allows for a detailed and thick analysis of the text yielding profound insights from the text, not by adding to but by drawing from the text itself. This rhetorical approach grows out of modern language theory and modern epistemology in an exercise of modern hermeneutics (Witherington, 2009b). This form of modern hermeneutics assists the researcher in discovering profound insights that can be appropriated to contemporary situations. This pressing the text for more can be an advance for theological and practical insights from the Christian Scriptures especially when applied to specific pericopes.

The Process in the Pericope

This research examined the textual issue of leadership in this pericope and its appropriation to the contemporary context. In this study are both the in the text issues of understanding leadership through this inductive analysis of the text and in front of the text issues of how it is to be applied in a present context for organizational and church leadership. Therefore, leadership in this study was examined from a theological perspective, but also from an anthropological perspective as well as a sociological perspective in setting the text in the context of specific people in a specific time and culture. This research applied socio-rhetorical interpretation to the texts in 1 Peter and related pericopes. This approach brought detailed attention to the text itself while bringing the rich resources of modern anthropology and sociology to the interpretation of the text (Robbins, 1996). So, this research brought attention to the text and viewed the realities related therein through the multiple textures not only of the text itself but through the lenses of anthropology and sociology as well.

There was not an easy approach here straight to application. First, the text must be examined in its textures inclusive of its context to find the real nature of the understanding of leadership that was intended. It is not possible to ferret out the meaning of the text while ignoring the genre signals in the document or the historical issues which leads to various kinds of misinterpretations (Witherington, 2009b). If the writer of Scripture leaves much unexpressed, this does not mean that the reader can create meaning, rather the writer assumes a presupposition pool common with his or her reader, which includes an encyclopedic understanding of various issues such as issues of society, linguistics, and rhetoric (Turner, 2000). This is the reason that the text must be examined in its various textures for deep accurate understanding of the text. Then, once understood, it can be brought into the present to be appropriated into the current context of organizations, churches, and leadership. The task of hermeneutics is to find contemporary relevance from the ancient texts and the reason one must not begin in the here and now is that the proper way of interpretation is to be found in the original intent of the biblical text; the key is to learn to read the text carefully and ask the right questions of the text (Fee & Stuart, 1993).

However, this study confined itself to the study of leadership in the Christian Scriptures from or in relationship to the writings in the document of 1 Peter. Though there are many other places and persons that address leadership in the Hebrew and Christian Scriptures, the scope of this study was narrowed to provide both depth and specific issues for comparison with other theories of leadership.

There are many reasons that this section of text needs to be explored for leadership studies. Other sections of the Christian Scriptures have been explored concerning the topic of leadership but in large part these have been in the writings of Paul and the gospels. Interestingly, it was Peter that Jesus spoke very directly to—even privately—about leadership, yet these sections have not been deeply explored. In addition, 1 Peter speaks directly to leaders about leadership much like Paul speaks to leaders in the Pastoral Epistles, yet the Petrine texts have not been mined for understanding like those of Paul. There is no need for competition here but simply a need for a thorough examination of the text that may have been neglected in leadership studies. In addition, there are ontological issues discussed in these writings that have ramifications for leadership that may not be discussed in other texts and rarely discussed in contemporary leadership research.

This study was limited to the writings of Peter in 1 Peter with no examination of 2 Peter or Peter's sermons in the book of Acts or consideration of the likelihood of the gospel of Mark coming from the preaching of Peter. For a complete consideration of the Petrine teachings, these other pericopes would have to be considered. The scope of this study was purposefully narrow to add to the present knowledge of textual study of Christian Scripture concerning leadership and as a foundation or exploratory study for further research into Petrine teachings concerning leadership and its application to contemporary contexts.

A good interpretation of the Scriptures will survive a close reading of the text.
Brian Russell

CHAPTER 3

SOCIO-RHETORICAL EXAMINATION AND INTERPRETATION

Socio-rhetorical interpretation is a method of examination of texts that is a close examination of the text in discovering different textures of texts in biblical interpretation. This approach invites detailed attention to the text itself while moving interactively into the world of the people who wrote them and into the present world (Robbins, 1996). This task of exegesis is to find out what was the original intent of the words of the text and the key is to learn to read the text carefully (Fee & Stuart, 1993). This careful reading of the text yields a thick texture from the Scriptures for interpretation. A nuanced understanding of the meaning of each passage demands a wide-ranging and multi-disciplined analysis or thick description of the text (Turner, 2000). Socio-rhetorical criticism brings together the contributions of literary criticism, social—scientific criticism, rhetorical criticism, post-modern criticism, and theological criticism into an integrated multilayered approach (Robbins, 1996). This integrated approach to textual analysis brings a shift in the way one perceives the text; the text is not merely a window through which to see meaning but now the focus is on the several layers within the text as the key to interpretation (Bekker, 2005). This approach yields clear yet multifaceted data for interpretation of the text.

This exploration of multiple layers in the text involves five different aspects: (a) inner texture, (b) intertexture, (c) social and cultural texture, (d) ideological texture, and (e) sacred texture (Robbins, 1996). In each of these five aspects is a further division of the interpretive process. Socio-rhetorical interpretation is a multidimensional approach to texts guided by a multidimensional hermeneutic; it is an interpretive analytic meaning that these methods and results are always under scrutiny (Robbins, 2004). These aspects or dimensions facilitate interpretation of the text but only as it proceeds from a close reading of the text in the different categories. This scrutiny helps to develop proper and profound understanding of the text in light of cultural, historical, rhetorical, anthropological, and literary reality. This process is multifaceted but not simply subject to the interpreter, it is subject to the text and context.

This study of rhetorical conventions may tune the ear of the interpreter to powerful overtones in the text that had not previously been suspected (Turner, 2000). However, there are presently different kinds of socio-rhetorical interpretation in use today in the understanding of biblical texts. One is a more historical enterprise analyzing the documents on the basis of ancient Greco-Roman rhetoric answering the question of how the biblical authors may have used rhetoric (Witherington, 2009b). One form called social—scientific criticism is the exegetical task of examining the social and cultural dimensions of the text and its environmental context through the utilization of the perspectives of the social sciences; it studies conditioning factors and intended consequences of the communication process and the text was designed as a vehicle to serve as an instrument of social, literary, and theological consequence (Elliot, 1993). Another approach grows out of modern language theory and modern epistemology in the understanding of texts and meaning seeking to apply rhetorical categories to the text in an exercise of modern hermeneutics (Witherington, 2009b). This last approach is the approach that is used in this exegetical research concerning leadership in 1 Peter. One of the notable contributions of this form of socio-rhetorical criticism is to bring literary criticism, social—scientific criticism, rhetorical criticism, post modern criticism, and theological criticism together into an integrated approach bringing that which is often separated together with the goal of being intricately sensitive to detail while being perceptively attentive to large fields of meaning (Robbins, 1996). This type of socio-rhetorical interpretation brings together both micro and macro worlds for interpretation that is both accurate and nuanced to answer the complicated and complex questions of reality.

This socio-rhetorical interpretation has been effective in exegetical work and interpretation of texts in other important explorations for leadership studies. Bekker (2006, 2007b) explored the hymn of Philippians 2:11-14 using socio-rhetorical analysis in developing the contemporary theory of kenotic leadership. In addition, Danley (2009) expanded the theory of kenotic leadership through applying socio-rhetorical interpretation in the same pericope. Self (2009) applied socio-rhetorical analysis in her exploration of 1 Corinthians 13 in connection to love and organizational leadership, and Zarate (2009) applied socio-rhetorical interpretation to Matthew 4 and 5 of the Christian Scriptures in examining the leadership of Jesus. Each of these research studies have expanded and nuanced the understanding of leadership in the contemporary context from the perspective of the Christian Scriptures, but none have examined the writings and teachings of Peter as found in 1 Peter. Socio-rhetorical interpretation, as described by Robbins (1996), was used in this study in light of its effective use in other studies of this nature and its ability to develop multiple textures in the text for a nuanced understanding of this pericope of the Christian Scriptures.

Need for Leadership

The contemporary need for good leadership in all different levels of society is evidenced by the focus on leadership studies in the last 50 years as well as the scandals that have proceeded from leaders in recent history. Leadership has been a topic of study for social scientists for much of the 20th century with no consensus on the definition of leadership except that it involves influence to accomplish group or organizational objectives. And, though there is diversity across cultures, it is expected that some aspects of leadership are universal (House et al., 2004). The question is how these universal aspects of leadership can be discovered since all social research must be done in the context of a particular culture. They can be compared for similarities, but can they definitively answer the universal question?

It is further complicated by the issues of human frailty and the context of contemporary society. Whereas a combination of faith, character, and virtue was the rock on which traditional leadership was founded, each of these has crumbled in contemporary society and been replaced with a craze for power and where style or presentation has become the new norm (Guinness, 2000). The examination of effective human leadership is set in the present context of individuals who have lost their bearings leading others. The way ahead must include new insights for leadership in spite of the present context of individuals and society.

Part of the solution may be looking back into history in addition to looking broadly across present cultures and human societies. It is presumptuous to act as if leadership philosophy was born in the 20th century; leadership theory is firmly grounded in the archives of history (Galbraith & Galbraith, 2004). History contains not only examples of leadership, but writings and ponderings about leadership from Plato's *Republic* of the Greek world to the Hebrew and Christian Scriptures of the Hebrew and Roman world. In the Golden Age of history, most scholars were convinced that everything must be understood in terms of development or historically but many have challenged that understanding of history; however, there is a real linkage between past, present, and future with every important discovery made about the past effecting the present and the future resulting in a historic study of life (Breisach, 2007). The study of history impacts present human reality and the future, as well, this includes issues of leadership models, theory, and principles.

In addition, spirituality is a key component in research concerning human life. There has been a turn to spirituality at the turn of the century in leadership studies (Bekker, 2007a). This spiritual component is becoming particularly apparent in leadership studies in this century with a new interests in the spiritual aspect of life and its effect on leadership and leadership theory as seen in spiritual leadership (Fry, 2003), kenotic leadership (Bekker, 2006), and authentic leadership (Klenke, 2007), as well as others (Patterson, 2003; Winston, 2002). This spiritual component can be seen and described in the writings of different world religions. Of particular interest in these theories and the present research is that of Christian spirituality as found in the Christian Scriptures. These texts speak directly and implicitly to the issue of leadership and its application in society. It is in this context that this study endeavored to combine Christian Scripture and history in addressing the issues of leadership in all of the complexity of human frailty for a nuanced understanding of leadership that can be applied to contemporary contexts. This study used Robbins (1996) socio-rhetorical interpretation to develop the texture of 1 Peter in understanding leadership from this text then compared these findings to kenotic leadership which was also developed through socio-rhetorical interpretation of a different pericope of Christian Scripture. In addition, these findings were compared to authentic leadership which was developed through social research.

This document (1 Peter) is an ad hoc pastoral document, and even the theological discussions present serve as the undergirding for the ethics, values, virtues, practices being inculcated by the author.
Ben Witherington III

CHAPTER 4

PRELIMINARY RESEARCH IN PETER

Since there has not been an abundance of research on the area of leadership in 1 Peter, this is an area where more exploration and research is needed. The present research concerning 1 Peter is focused on theological issues and content, with a focus on suffering and practical living (Davids, 1990; Elliot, 2007; Green, 2007; Grudem, 1999; Hiebert, 1992; Jobes, 2005; Luther, 1990; Marshall, 1991; Seagraves, 2010; Witherington, 2007). Some of the practical living content is focused on instructions to leaders in a section of Chapter 5. In the context of these studies, none of them have used Robbins' (1996) socio-rhetorical method of interpretation in their exegetical processes.

A search of dissertations yielded thousands of studies on Peter and 1 Peter, focusing on theological or hermeneutical issues or how to live in the midst of suffering, a main theme in this text. Nevertheless, there was not a single dissertation on leadership issues in 1 Peter. Attention to the gospels and the Pauline literature has tended to dominate the scholarly scene and have left 1 Peter and other writings in a kind of canonical "twilight zone," where it has been treated as an exegetical stepchild (Elliot, 2007). However, there have been some recent studies on the leadership of Peter and 1 Peter; though these are not dissertations, they are a beginning for research (Faulhaber, 2007; Leahy, 2010; Spencer, 2008). Faulhaber used socio-rhetorical interpretation in the text of 1 Peter studying the transformative process necessary for creating innovative organizations by focusing on the nuances of spiritual transformation and character development in the context of transformational leadership used by Peter. Faulhaber concluded that in this text, Peter's authentic transformational leadership influences the community by having the character of Christ. Leahy examined Peter as a model of leadership by examining his progression of leadership from John 21 to the writing of 1 Peter. Leahy used socio-rhetorical analysis of 1 Peter 5 in showing Peter as having the characteristics of charismatic, transformational, and servant leadership. Spencer used a phenomenological approach to examine the experiences of Peter in his formation as a leader. Spencer, in his examination of 1 Peter, found significant statements for the definition and operationalization of leadership, formulating several meanings for leadership including transformative influence. These studies are unique in their focus on the leadership of Peter and the use of socio-rhetorical interpretation in their examination of the text. Though these studies are not dissertations, their research and conclusions are worthy of consideration and examination in developing an understanding of principles of leadership as found in the text of 1 Peter.

Though these studies are few and limited, they come from a growing body of work concerning the Hebrew and Christian Scriptures and the ramifications of these texts for leadership studies (Ayers, 2006; Bekker, 2006; Danley, 2009; Gray, 2008; Hardgrove, 2008, Niewold, 2006; Self, 2009; Winston, 2002; Zarate, 2009). This research has increased recently in an endeavor to find principles of leadership as contained in these sacred texts as a foundation for leadership in ecclesial as well as organizational settings outside of the church. The study of leadership is concerned with the understanding of reality, the pursuit of how the world actually operates, and how spirituality deeply informs this kind of leadership approach (Bekker, 2007a). Bekker (2008) provided a reflection on some of the 21st-century approaches to Christian leadership that used approaches of examining biblical leaders and exegetical approaches of the Hebrew and Christian Scriptures while comparing them to modern theories of leadership. He concluded that the turn of the century brought a new era of academic exploration to the quest to define Christian leadership, yet calling for more work to be done since many of the forms of Christian leadership had not been explored yet. This burgeoning area of study needs new deeper exploration of the form of Christian leadership as lived and developed by Peter.

Concerning the text of 1 Peter, most of the attention for leadership studies has been on the pericope of 1 Peter 5:1-7 wherein Peter gave direct instructions to church leaders about leadership in the church. Reading between the lines one can form the idea of what the duties of the leaders were, but the main point is the way leadership was exercised in that overseeing the flock is paramount and the character description of what it takes to be a leader is following the example of Christ (Witherington, 2007). The exhortation of Peter in this text is directly to leaders concerning the ontology as well as the behavior of a leader. Peter began this chapter with instructions to guiding the behavior of leaders, but not as ones with special privilege. He presented less formalized roles and practices of leadership, but where the character of the leader is paramount (Green, 2007). These directions came from Peter as their leader who learned of leadership from Jesus in the gospels in following His example and receiving His teaching concerning leadership. Peter exhorted the elders using the same verb that Jesus used when He told Peter to tend His sheep in John 21. Now Peter was applying what he had learned and lived to the leaders who were overseers of the flock. Peter's exhortation to the leaders is simple: to shepherd the flock of God. This is a concept from the Hebrew Scriptures and he called himself a fellow elder, stressing his empathy with them, rather than a position over them, and avoiding the use of exalted titles (Davids, 1990). Peter's exhortation was not so much about the office of a leader but of the person who leads, and Peter set the example as Christ set the example for Peter and for other leaders. In this passage, Peter gave instructions about the type of shepherd leadership that is needed; that the leaders must oversee the church in a godly way, shepherding the flock rather than domineering it (Jobes, 2005). It is not the details about the behavior of the leader that are emphasized but the way of not domineering as a leader that is important here. Then there are specific functions or contrasts that are given to the leaders in clarifying this process of leading without domineering.

Peter identified the elders as shepherds then qualified the exercise of oversight with three antitheses: (a) not under coercion, but voluntarily in a godly way; (b) not greedily but freely; and (c) not as those who lord it over others but as examples to the flock (Green, 2007). Peter described for the leaders three sins to which leaders are prone and the corresponding antidotes to which they should give attention

(Grudem, 1999). These three antidotes then give a positive instruction of the way of leadership for these leaders. Peter was telling the leaders of the church exactly what the Lord told him in taking care of the sheep and that the role of the leader is deeply rooted in the Hebrew Scriptures and takes its essential character from the nature of God and this leadership is realized in the embodiment of the character of Christ (Green, 2007). The focus of this exhortation is imitating the Lord in specific ways of leadership that are both counterintuitive and counter cultural.

In his research, Spencer (2008) examined Peter as a writer and author and the implications for leadership as found in 1 Peter as can be seen in Tables 1-3.

Table 1: Peter as Writer, Leadership Definitions

Item	Verse	Statement
1	1 Peter 1:1	Peter, an apostle (one that is sent)
2	1 Peter 1:2	Elect (ones that are chosen lead by intent of God)
3	1 Peter 2:5	A spiritual house
4	1 Peter 2:5	A holy priesthood
5	1 Peter 2:9	A chosen generation
6	1 Peter 2:9	A royal priesthood
7	1 Peter 2:9	A holy nation, God's own special people
8	1 Peter 2:21	Leaving an example that you should follow in his steps (leaders as examples)
9	1 Peter 5:2	Shepherd the flock of God (metaphor for leadership)
10	1 Peter 5:2	Serving as overseers (synonym for leadership)
11	1 Peter 5:3	Not as being lords over those entrusted to you but being examples

Note. Adapted from *Peter: A Phenomenology of Leadership*, by J. L. Spencer, 2008, Paper presented at Biblical Perspectives in Leadership Research Roundtable, Virginia Beach, Virginia, p. 22. Copyright 2008 by J. L. Spencer.

Table 2: Peter as Writer, Leader Operationalizations

Item	Verse	Statement
1	1 Peter 2:5	Offer up spiritual sacrifices
2	1 Peter 2:9	Proclaim the praises of Him
3	1 Peter 3:18	Christ also suffered once for sins (cost of leadership)
4	1 Peter 5:2	(Do not shepherd) by compulsion but willingly
5	1 Peter 5:2	(Do not shepherd) for dishonest gain but eagerly

Note. Adapted from *Peter: A Phenomenology of Leadership,* by J. L. Spencer, 2008, Paper presented at Biblical Perspectives in Leadership Research Roundtable, Virginia Beach, Virginia, p. 23. Copyright 2008 by J. L. Spencer.

Table 3: Peter as Writer, Formulated Meanings

Item	About	Meanings
1	Leadership	The transformative influence toward others with longevity and consistency
2	Leadership	A calling of directing lives toward godly transformation
3	Leadership	Designated and authorized by God to represent Him and His purposes
4	Leadership	Metaphorically seen as shepherds, priests, overseers, and servants
5	Leaders	Fulfill key role in modeling action for followers to see and emulate
6	Leaders	Direct followers to specific actions and behaviors to acquire a preferred future
7	Leaders	Remind followers of their expected responsibilities and the sacrifices involved
8	Leaders	Communicate with followers with written systematic instructions

| 9 | Leaders | Inform and teach followers using special information received |

Note. Adapted from *Peter: A Phenomenology of Leadership,* by J. L. Spencer, 2008, Paper presented at Biblical Perspectives in Leadership Research Roundtable, Virginia Beach, Virginia, pp. 25-26. Copyright 2008 by J. L. Spencer.

Based upon these findings in the text of Peter, Spencer (2008) defined *leadership* as the authorized calling and influence to transform others and the ability to inform, inspire, and protect followers. This leadership is operationalized by establishing clear directives and associated behaviors as well as exemplifying a reproducible model for leader and follower development (Spencer, 2008). There are two notes that are important in this particular study. First, it is part of a larger study and while the focus was on Peter and leadership, it was broader in that it included research in the Gospels and Acts as well as 2 Peter, so some of the conclusions could have been influenced by this perspective. Second, and more importantly, this is a significant study in that it viewed leadership from 1 Peter as a complete text rather than just a small section in Chapter 5 of 1 Peter.

Faulhaber (2007) examined the entire text of 1 Peter finding Peter's leadership as both similar to and distinct from authentic transformational leadership with the distinctions based in the fact that the motivation for this type of leadership was found in Christ and not in Peter as the leader. However, there were many similarities. In this context, the authentic transformational leader will have (a) idealized influence that comes from Christ, (b) inspirational motivation that provides a compelling vision of the Christian praising and glorifying God by standing in holiness and overcoming tribulation, (c) intellectual stimulation by sparking creativity and innovation, and (d) consideration by using power to help others become leaders as well as creating cultures where charity is the norm (Faulhaber, 2007). This research is significant in that it uses socio-rhetorical interpretation in an endeavor to understand leadership principles in 1 Peter as a complete text not just the short pericope in 1 Peter Chapter 5.

First Peter is a document that is largely practical in nature and ethical in content, though it includes theology (Witherington, 2007). In this document, there is a rhetorical strategy to give the recipients the assurance that God consistently transforms disgrace into grace and shame into honor and it is the first document of the Christian Scriptures to address the Christian community's relation to the larger community (Elliot, 2007). This relation to the larger community contains practical instructions concerning several issues for the believers in living as resident aliens in the context of the community concerning authority, suffering, and leadership. First Peter reflects the larger macrostructures of rhetoric and like other New Testament documents looks like a rhetorical speech wherein rhetoric is the art of persuasion (Witherington, 2009a). The rhetoric of 1 Peter is shown in Figure 1.

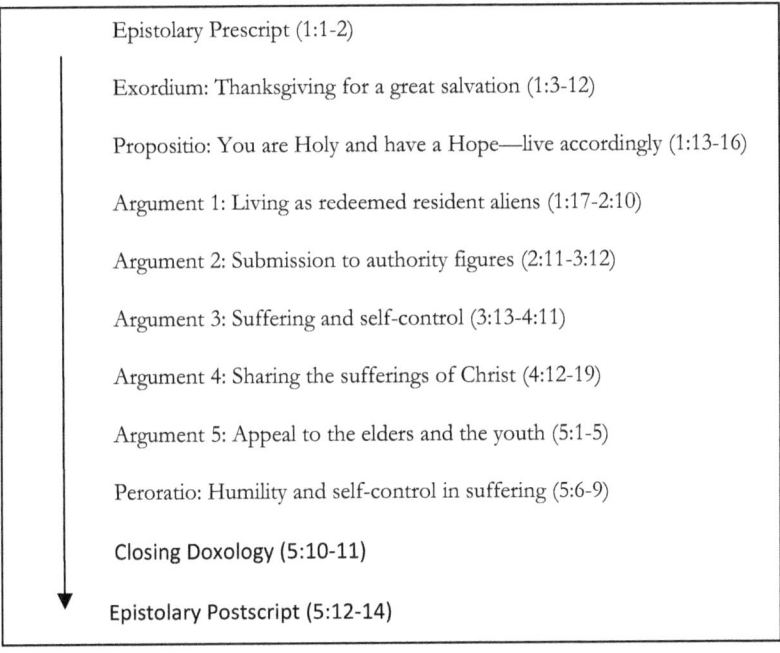

Figure 1: The rhetoric of First Peter. Reprinted from *Letters and Homilies for Hellenized Christians: A Socio-Rhetorical Commentary on 1-2 Peter* (p. 49), by B. Witherington, 2007, Downers Grove, IL: InterVarsity Press. Copyright 2007 by B. Witherington.

This rhetorical structure clearly communicates Peter's intent to persuade the recipients of the letter in several areas including that of authority and concerning leaders in the church. In the study of

1 Peter is found the fact that the author is constructing a rhetorical world; a world of advice and persuasion where certain beliefs and behaviors are inculcated for social as well as theological and ideological reasons (Witherington, 2009a). This pericope must then be interpreted in light of this rhetorical world examining this advice and persuasive instruction by the author.

The fact that this Petrine letter is addressed to an area in which both Pauline and Johannine traditions were strong shows that Peter's importance for the church was acknowledged in the early stages of the church, First Peter should be seen as evidence for the universalizing of Peter as a leader for the whole church (Perkins, 2000). Peter is acknowledged as leader among the early church at large, though he writes this letter to a specific group. Peter was the great bridge figure between the ministry of Jesus and the rise and ministry of the early church which he helped set in motion; this document therefore merits close scrutiny since it has a clear link with the Jesus movement—Jesus Himself (Witherington, 2009b). First Peter is a general epistle written to dozens of churches scattered throughout four Roman provinces in Asia Minor and Peter assumed that all of these churches, whether founded by Paul or others, whether Gentile or Jewish, would have elders ruling them (Grudem, 1994). He spoke with authority and direction to all of these churches.

Peter's exhortation concerning leadership used the image of shepherd similar to the image used by Jesus in commissioning Peter in John 21:15-19, of a shepherd that undergoes suffering. This picture is seen again in 1 Peter as Peter exhorted the leaders to follow Christ in suffering and shepherding in anticipating the glory to come (Perkins, 2000). Perkins declared that the exhortation that constitutes the body of 1 Peter indicated the kind of caring that needs to be done for the flock in leading as a shepherd. The text is an exhortation to leaders to follow the example of Christ, not Peter, in suffering in the process of leading the people of God as a shepherd to them.

Anderson (1997) observed that of the three biblical models of leadership the most prominent one is that of shepherd as seen in the Hebrew Scriptures as well as described by Peter in his exhortation to leaders to follow the example of the Chief Shepherd, Jesus, in leadership found in 1 Peter 5. This model of shepherd leadership is the way of Christian leadership even in the modern world and these leaders become effective through loving service and authentic relationships; they are committed enough to put their lives on the line for those they lead (Anderson, 1997). This shepherd leadership, as promoted by Peter, was based upon the leadership found in the Hebrew Scriptures as well as the teaching of Jesus to the apostles. After modeling shepherd leadership, Jesus passed the model on to the apostles, particularly Peter in exhorting him to feed the sheep in John 21:15-17, and in essence exhorting him to adopt Jesus' style of leadership (Anderson, 1997). This shepherding style of leadership was given with specific instructions in 1 Peter 5. According to Anderson, there is a relational basis for shepherding that requires availability, trust, and commitment. This form of leadership has a long history but a practical relevant application to contemporary leadership in that this shepherd metaphor was passed on to us intentionally (Anderson, 1997).

The document of 1 Peter is a pastoral document with theological discussions serving as foundations for ethics, values, virtues, and practices with the outworking advice about rulers, masters, wives, elders, and young men in constructing the Christian household (Witherington, 2007). This construction has advice that intersects with leadership issues that are both implicit and explicit. Witherington (2009b) observed that Peter had a robust ecclesiology in this text referring to the people as resident aliens who are called to become the house of God and the priests within it while he is constructing a rhetorical world of advice, consent, and persuasion to inculcate beliefs and behaviors for theological and ideological reasons. In 1 Peter 5 comes a section about leadership functions in spite of the fact that all are priests there are particular persons being singled out for leadership positions who were to follow the example of Christ in the way of exercising leadership (Witherington, 2009b). Witherington (2007) stated that these leaders were to lead according to their grace gifts in tending the flock of God using the image of shepherd as portrayed by Christ as the Chief Shepherd and to include humility. Leadership, then, is a form of service with humility and the basic sense of the word is to be base-minded or have the mind of a servant (Witherington, 2007). Peter's understanding of leadership included the unique gifting of the person coupled with humility in following the example of Christ, the ultimate leader and shepherd.

Nevertheless, it is not only the image of shepherd that is found in this text as a description of leadership, there are others that need consideration. One description is that of priesthood that Peter used twice in rapid succession. In 1 Peter 2:9, the believers are called a royal priesthood, quoting exactly from the LXX of Exodus 19:6 where God promises this status to all in Israel that keep His covenant (Grudem, 1999). One cannot escape the impression that Peter clearly intended to establish a parallel between Israel and the church (Hiebert, 1992). In Exodus 19, the royal priesthood is in relation to the rest of the earth; Israel was to play a mediating role between God and the nations (Jobes, 2005). In Exodus, all Israelites were invited to become priests but they did not because of disobedience, whereas in 1 Peter all believers are invited into the priesthood and can become priests. All who come to Christ are a holy priesthood able to draw near to God and offer spiritual sacrifices; now there is no longer an elite priesthood with special privileges and claims of special access to God (Grudem, 1999). The people are a royal priesthood that constitutes a group of priests belonging to a king, and each priest is a person who serves God and can intercede on behalf of others (Marshall, 1991). In Israel, all were called to be priests but they could not, now in the context of Christ all believers become priests with the vocation to intercede for others and the injunction live and behave in such a way as to lead others to glorify God. In addition to the image of priesthood, is the specific instruction concerning authority and one's relationship to kings and governors that have authority in human institutions. The instruction here is to be subject to authority—toward all forms of rightful human authority—and has broad application to civil government, masters, and slaves, as well as husbands and wives because God has established such patterns of authority for the orderly function of human life (Grudem, 1999). Peter was dealing with the interface between individual Christians and pagan society (Witherington, 2007). Authority is addressed directly and is clearly seen as an issue of leadership, not just in the church but in the context of society generally.

It is significant that the leaders are to set the example for the people and that Jesus is held out as the ultimate example to be followed. In Chapter 2, there is some interesting language to describe the example of Christ, using the term for the exact pattern of letters so that children could copy them or trace them so as to learn the letters. It also uses the image of literally following in someone's footsteps; this was the essence of ancient education (Witherington, 2007). Christ and elders lead by example and the followers imitated closely so as to learn and grow. Then by following the example of Christ, one comes to Him as Shepherd and Guardian of one's soul. The term *overseer* here means to look at, to care for, or to oversee, and it stresses active and responsible care (Hiebert, 1992). Jesus then is seen as the leader in 1 Peter who leads by example as well as by overseeing and shepherding. Green (2007) outlined a chiastic structure with instructions to everyone, followed by instructions to slaves with the example of Christ as the pivot of the chiasm, followed by instruction for wives, then instruction for everyone. This structure can be seen in Figure 2, clearly showing that Peter focused on Christ as the example in issues of submission, authority, and leadership.

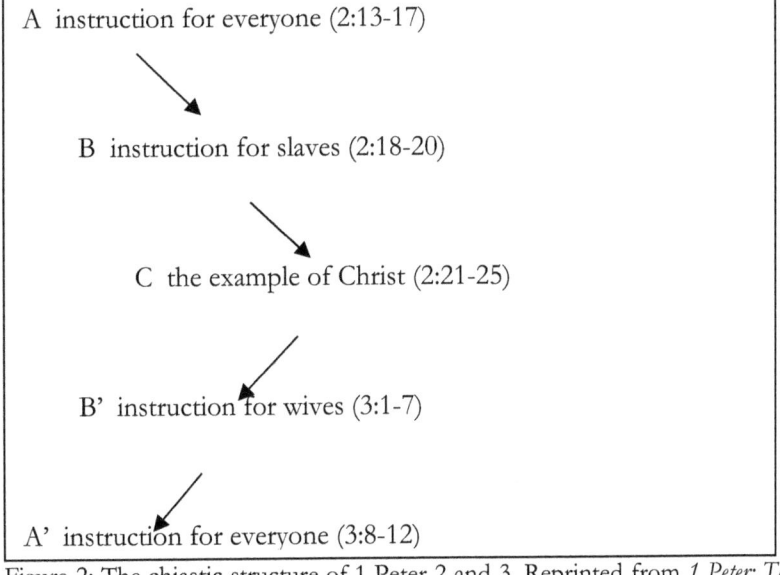

Figure 2: The chiastic structure of 1 Peter 2 and 3. Reprinted from *1 Peter: The Two Horizons New Testament Commentary* (p. 72), by J. Greene, 2007, Grand Rapids, MI: William B. Eerdmans. Copyright 2007 by J. Greene.

Early research on religious leadership focused on Jesus as a leader (Weber, 1968), but with no reference to Peter or his leadership. This early research was sociological in nature and was revisited by McClymond (2001) later, but still in a sociological context in examining charismatic leadership. Early research on 1 Peter focused on the theology of the text especially in connection to Christian life and suffering issues. Polycarp and Irenaus, 2nd-century church leaders, both used 1 Peter in their writings and Luther in the 16th-century wrote a commentary on 1 Peter as did Calvin in the same time period.

Commentaries have continued to be written into the 21st century with the aforementioned focus on theology. However, with this turn to spirituality in leadership studies has come many leadership studies based in exegetical work but with few focused on the writings of Peter. This paucity of research on 1 Peter and leadership calls for a further examination of the text of 1 Peter for the understanding of leadership principles as found in this pericope of Christian Scripture.

Leadership principles from 1 Peter can be seen in an examination of the text of 1 Peter. While there is a great amount of exegetical work on the text of 1 Peter, it is generally focused on the theological and practical issues of suffering and living in the context of a hostile environment. However, there is some research in 1 Peter 5 that speaks directly about leadership in the first five verses, but there is even fewer that address leadership in the context of the full text of 1 Peter for a more developed concept of leadership as taught by Peter in the Christian Scriptures.

In the writing of 1 Peter, leadership is compared to that of a shepherd, exemplified by Christ, and seen in relationship to submission and authority. However, there are further issues for leadership that proceed from the concept of priesthood. In addition, the leaders are given specific instructions by Peter concerning their role as examples, their motive in leading, and in resisting the temptations of greed. Examining the book of 1 Peter as a whole provides a way to more fully grasp the teaching of Peter concerning leadership.

A cross-disciplinary approach that integrates current social definitions and theories of leadership demonstrates that the Pauline model of leadership as propagated in Paul's letters to the Philippians is a valid model for leadership study and application.
David R. Gray

CHAPTER 5

PRELIMINARY RESEARCH IN PAUL'S WRITINGS (PHILIPPIANS 2:5-11)

Kenotic leadership is a model of leadership developed from an examination of a Pauline pericope of Christian Scripture in Philippians 2:5-11. In defining a "proto-theory" of Christian leadership, the text of the Philippian hymn was examined resulting in a proposal of a model of leadership that included (a) Christological mimesis, (b) kenosis (self-emptying), (c) servant posturing, (d) humane orientation, (e) active humility, and (f) missional obedience (Bekker, 2009). This model proposed an imitation or mimesis of Jesus Christ in His way of leadership through kenosis or self-emptying that involves one becoming a servant—a humane orientation with active humility and obedience. This model affects both the ontology of a person—who one is—and becoming a servant, as well as humility, and the behavior of the person—what one does in acts of obedience. Paul's purpose in this text was to persuade believers to be humble and put the interests of others first and hold up the example of Christ who gave up the status and privilege of heaven (Grudem, 1994). This is the imitation of Christ in the process of kenosis or kenotic leadership.

This pericope of Philippians 2:5-7 has been clearly identified as a hymn and these types of communal hymns were used in teaching and the formation of members; this hymn began with a call to imitation based on the values and behavior of Jesus Christ (Bekker, 2008). This call to "imitate" Jesus, who is then shown to be Divine in this text, was then a call to imitate God with a surprising call to imitate the humble crucified Savior using a *cursus pudorum* rather than to imitate the glories of the Roman Emperor with a *cursus honorum* (Bekker, 2007b). The way or flow of ignominy or humiliation and shame as exemplified by Christ and as proposed to be imitated by leaders, has five components in this pericope. The leaders voluntarily moves from a place of privilege by kenosis, servant posturing, embracing humanity, humility, and obedience, after which there is a status reversal through divine exaltation in the imitation of Christ (Bekker, 2007b). The example of Christ in this hymn sets the way of leadership for the Christian leader who is to imitate this process of the way of ignominy.

In Christian theology, kenosis is the concept of the self-emptying of one's own will and becoming entirely receptive and responsible to God's perfect will and Jesus Christ is the example of this process in Philippians 2:5-11 (Danley, 2009). Kenosis denotes self-limitation wherein Christ emptied Himself; though He pre-existed in the form of God, Christ did not count that being on an equality with God as a prize which He must not let slip, but emptied Himself, taking the form of a servant (Berkhof, 1996). This self-emptying took on concrete ways of living and leading on the life of Christ which the leader is encouraged to imitate. Specifically, the word kenosis is translated in Philippians 2:7 as "made of Himself nothing," and is from the root word meaning "to empty," and it includes all of the details of the humiliation which follow (Hardgrove, 2008). Christ did not empty Himself of anything, He simply emptied Himself; he poured Himself out by taking on the form of a slave which means to become powerless or emptied of significance (Fee, 1995). Kenotic Christology is the view drawn from the Christian Scriptures such as Philippians 2:7, that in becoming incarnate the second person of the Trinity somehow emptied Himself in order to become truly human (Crisp, 2007). This process of kenosis in Philippians serves as an exemplum and a focus in what this would mean in an alternate vision of Christian leadership, opening the door to explore the values of the radical giving up of status and privilege in leadership through a mystical union with Christ leading to personal transformation of both the leaders and the follower (Bekker, 2006). Kenosis is explained as the way of leadership of Jesus Christ and held out as an example for other leaders to follow. The purpose of Paul's use of the hymn was to challenge believers to follow the example of Jesus, to empty themselves of envy, selfish ambition, and conceit, and be filled instead with the attitude of Christ in self-renunciation, humility, obedience, and service (Hardgrove, 2008). This is a most striking phrase that has no parallel in the whole of Greek literature; it is suggested that this is a poetic way of saying that He poured himself out, putting Himself totally at the disposal of people (O'Brien, 1991). Christ emptied Himself; He effaced all thought of himself and poured out his fullness to enrich others. His actions could be described as setting aside His rights and not insisting on His own way (Hawthorne, 1983). This process of self-emptying then has not only negative but positive connotations of giving of self to others in various aspects. This process is a process of self-emptying that applies in very specific ways in the process of humiliation as exemplified by Christ as well as to leadership as modeled by Christ and endorsed by Paul.

In the Philippians hymn, Christ emptied Himself by taking the form of a slave, but it is important that this does not speak of mere service but the radical quest to take the form of a slave (Bekker, 2006). Unlike many oriental despots, the preexistent Christ, who already possessed equality with God, understood His position to mean giving instead of getting (O'Brien, 1991). This was a voluntary act by Christ in which He relinquished divine rights to take on the role of servant (Hardgrove, 2008). When leaders, having practiced kenosis, are able to enter the world of their followers and take the posture of servant, relationships of mutual healing and trust are formed that remove the social and power distance between them in mutual liberation and transformation (Bekker, 2007b). In kenotic leadership, the leader initiates the role of servant in the context of the relationships with followers, thereby bringing trust, mutuality, and transformation into the dynamic of leadership.

The next step in the hymn is that Jesus Christ was found in the form of a man. This word for "form" is used of persons of their outward appearance, form, or bearing (Friberg & Friberg, 2000). This term or word should be understood in the sense of Christ's full identity with the human race; He shared man's plight in reality (O'Brien, 1991). Reading this hymn as an ethical exemplum opens a new avenue for discussion of the social values that are proposed in the context of societies riddled with social inequalities, proposing a praxis of charity, identification with one being served, and of authentic love (Bekker, 2007b). Kenosis is a relinquishment of self for the sake of others in seeking right relationship; it is recognition of shared humanity with others (Reid, 2009). Jesus embraced His own humanity and the humanity of others. This word for "found" is passive in that it is to be found or to find to be or find oneself (Friberg & Friberg, 2000). The implication is that Jesus found Himself human but He did not grasp His equality with God, He took this form freely. This embracing of humanity then has implications for leaders to identify with followers by serving them in love in contradistinction to a self-focus of leadership.

Humility is the next step in this Philippian hymn wherein Christ humbled Himself. He set the example for others to humble instead of exalt themselves in the way or flow of leadership. This call to humility is not only the call to identify with humanity and servant posturing, it is the voluntary rejection of symbols and systems of power, prestige, and privilege (Bekker, 2006). It is a way of leading that is not focused on power, but its focus is on humility in the leader and becoming a servant to the followers. These are both issues of ontology with ramifications for leadership behavior that are counterculturalism in their original context as well the contemporary context. Some of the would-be leaders at Philippi were driven by selfish ambition with personal agendas that had less to do with humility than with pride and less to do with serving than being served (Hardgrove, 2008). In examining the local Christian community during the time of this writing, it was found that this church consisted of a cross-section of the stratified Roman society that was typical at that time and this hymn calls for an inversion in social values in the church that they saw around them in the socially competitive Roman community (Wortham, 1996). This exhortation offered a critique of the tyrannies of the timocratic leadership style of Roman Philippi offering an alternative vision of leadership (Bekker, 2007b). Humility became synonymous with the name of Jesus and central to the Christian ethic and Peter told these leaders they were to model virtue following their head Shepherd (Witherington, 2007). This is a call to humility in the exercise of leadership.

The final exhortation found in this pericope is that of obedience in that Christ obeyed even to the point of dying on a cross. Christ became subject to the law through His taking on the form of a man and in His entire life He was obedient in action and suffering to the point of a shameful death (Berkhof, 1996). His obedience included His death of the cross, the ultimate sacrifice. In the Philippian hymn this profound reality is held out as an example for the believers to follow. The practical application is clear, obedience and commitment to this alternative view of social order would bring dishonor in Roman Philippi but it would bring honor in Christ and in ultimate reality. This was a call to the believers to abandon the social implications of honor and shame and to follow the new way of leadership as set forth by Christ (Bekker, 2007b). Obedience was the ultimate act in Christ and now leaders must obey in developing humane-oriented, humble leadership rather than socially upward mobile culturally accepted standards of leadership and living.

The way back to paradise is by the way of the cross and the complete abandonment of self and individuals, like Christ, must empty themselves and not hold life as something to be grasped wherein this form of discipleship is for all believers, but in the case of those called to leadership it takes on an objectivity that confronts the whole church with the priority of Christ (Power, 1998). The leaders are examples of those who have embraced kenosis so that others can be confronted with this kenotic way of life and discipleship. The office of leadership constitutes a particular form of participation in the priesthood of Christ and, being true to its origins, the ministerial priesthood has no other function than to make itself disposable to this mission (Power, 1998). Leaders are those who lead the way in loving the church and the world through the process of kenosis in imitation of Christ.

Jesus brings a pattern of radical reversal of authority and power to those who are called to leadership; it is a pattern that completely undermines relationships of domination and control which have characterized human society by the pattern of Christ as a servant (Power, 1998). Kenosis is this radical reversal as seen in creation, the cross, and in Jesus Himself. This servant identity, self-emptying love, and commitment to the church brings a radicalism to the life and ministry of the ministerial priesthood as leaders in the community which mirrors to the world the very nature of God in kenosis and affirms the ontology of the priesthood not of sacred status but of sacred service (Power, 1998). In this sense, leadership is ontological in that the leader mimics Jesus not simply in His act of serving but in the self-emptying process to become an obedient servant. The leaders set the example for others to follow, not simply in the praxis of service, but in the process of kenosis which results in service. This is a radical reversal of leadership concepts in opposition to oppressive issues of power and authority but it involves a participation in the divine act of kenosis not simply involving a method of behavior.

Wright (1992) saw in this pericope a contrast between Adam wanting to be God in arrogance, and Christ in humility becoming human and this contrast is most effective if Christ is understood to have renounced the rank and privileges to which He had every right. The thrust of the passage is that the one who before becoming human possessed divine equality did not regard that status as something to exploit but instead interpreted it as a calling to obedient humiliation and death (Wright, 1992). This contrast and calling is the backdrop of this hymn about Christ with personal ramifications for the believers. This passage is well able to fulfill the role, which it has in Paul's developing argument that of the example which Christians are to imitate (Wright, 1992). This imitation is the imitation of Christ in His humility by not grasping His rightful rank and privilege. Martin (1997) saw the hymn as more of an exhortation to live under the Lordship of Christ rather than following the example of Christ, especially since the exaltation of Christ is detailed and not just His humiliation. Since no one else can be exalted as Lord, the example motif breaks down in the second part of the hymn. However, the point of the hymn could be to show the process of humility and its extreme case of Christ on the cross and the extreme case of exaltation in Christ being exalted as Lord. Neither position is available to mere humans, but the path of humility and path of God's favor are the endorsed path of the Christian life and Jesus has set the example. It says let this attitude be in you; the key focus is on attitude and imitation of the process not the exact events. This exhortation in Verse 5 reaches back to 2:2-4 for its definition and ahead to 2:6-8 for its illustration. He selects the qualities of the Lord that fit the needs of the Philippians, as being in the mind of Christ and which the Philippians were to include in their own spiritual lives—a spirit of humility, self-abnegation, and an interest in the welfare of others

(Wuest, 1966). The words *let mind be* are the translation of one Greek word which means to have understanding, to direct one's mind to a thing to strive for or to seek; the sum total of the thought is urging the Philippians to emulate in their lives the virtues of the Lord of an attitude of humility and self-abnegation for the benefit of others (Wuest, 1966). Even Martin saw this reality once the text is set in its contextual setting, though his focus was on obedience to Christ. In Philippians 2:1, the believers were reminded that their life together should be marked by what they have in common and the key to this moral incentive was their selfless regard for others and an active desire to promote their neighbor's interest in preference to their own and, above all, there was to be humility that was seen in Paul's telling the story of the Lord of glory who became servant of all (Martin, 1997).

This imitation or mimesis of the Lord is an important key to this section of the Philippian correspondence. It is imitation in humility as the process of becoming the person who is exalted by the Lord to their place of destiny. For Jesus, He is the Lord of the universe; for the Philippians, it is to their place of human destiny. A broad ranging school of thought has developed around the idea that the most important human motive is that of mimesis, which is not just the tendency to imitate others but to imitate their desires and that this process facilitates learning and empathy in individuals (Webb, 2009). In the imitation of Christ is the reformation of human nature through conformity with Christ and the notion of putting on Christ by mimesis of the perfect example is drawn from Pauline Epistles and Patristic thought (Herdt, 2008). This imitation of Christ is neither new nor novel but has permeated study of Scripture for centuries as a way of change that is ontological as well as counterintuitive. This mimetic process regards virtue as a finite reflection of God's infinite perfection and in this sense virtue is imitative while being reflective of the distinctiveness of each individual character (Herdt, 2008). Mimesis is a process that through imitation reflects imperfect finite virtue in response to God's infinite perfection. This is the process to which Paul refers in Philippians in his exhortation to Philippian leaders. The Christ-hymn presents Jesus as the supreme example of the humble, self-sacrificing, self-denying, self-giving service that Paul has been urging the

Philippians to practice and, therefore, this hymn presents Christ as the ultimate model for moral action with the exhortation for them to have this frame of mind wherein Christ is the illustration (Hawthorne, 1983).

The thrust of Paul's argument is that the Philippians needed to change their personal attitude by looking to Christ as the perfect example of virtuous behavior and they must respond to the leadership of Christ since ultimately a proper response to His leadership will be reflected in their leadership (Danley, 2009). It is about the life and leadership of Christ, but appropriately it is about an exhortation to proper leadership among the Philippians and by extension in the church. Paul wanted the Philippian church to recognize true authentic leadership through the lens of Christ's kenosis and the humility and commitment of service to others since Christ chose this position of humility to set a precedent for true leadership (Bekker, 2007b). This leadership was exemplified by Christ and then explained by Paul for the value that it would bring to leadership. Paul provided the ultimate leadership model of Christ, with a call for ethical virtues-based leadership behavior and a call to leaders to exercise humility with the result of a positive transformation of self, indicating transformative leadership principles (Bekker, 2007b). This theory is based on the leadership of Christ as the ultimate model for other leaders to follow in transformative leadership.

Kenotic leadership is a countercultural form of leadership based in a pericope of the Christian Scriptures as found in Philippians 2:5-11. The Philippians and we ourselves are not called upon to simply imitate God by what we do, but also to have this mind developed in us so that we bear God's image in our attitudes and relationships in the Christian community and beyond (Fee, 1995). In kenosis, the idea is to completely leave or eliminate high status or rank and here the king of creation becomes a mere human leaving behind all privilege subject to weakness; in contrast to Adam and Eve who showed the dark side of leadership, Jesus showed the path to kenotic leadership (Hjalmarson, 2006). This hymn presents Jesus as the supreme example of humble, self-sacrificing, self-giving service that Paul had been urging the believers to practice in their relations with each other. Christ is set forth as the ultimate model for Christian behavior and action (O'Brien, 1991). Paul's motive was not theological but ethical, in giving instruction on Christian living not on doctrine, but presenting Christ as the ultimate model (Hawthorne, 1983). This was modeled by and endorsed to the believers by Paul as the proper way or flow of leadership. This model can continue to be used in contemporary settings but it is still countercultural. This status does not mean it would not be effective; in fact it could facilitate effectiveness in the contemporary setting. Kenosis can be applied to social contexts which have a propensity for deadlock over issues of equality with kenosis providing a way beyond the impasse over competing rights (Reid, 2009). This is an issue for leadership in the developing forward movement in the social context of organizations. Kenotic leadership encourages the imitation of Christ in the way He lived and lead. This way of leadership led to exaltation in the person of Christ and could also lead to this same status reversal for those who imitate Him. These injunctions affirm that in the divine order of things, self-humbling leads inevitably to exaltation and this is applicable not only to Christ but also to Christians (Hawthorne, 1983). The irony is that the status that was originally sought by Roman leaders and by contemporary leaders is actually found in a countercultural and counterintuitive way of leadership as seen in kenotic leadership.

The kenotic leadership theory has been developed by an examination of the Christian Scriptures from Philippians 2:4-7. This concept for leadership is based on the example of Christ as explained and detailed in this pericope of Scripture. The model calls for the leader to follow the example of Christ or to have the same attitude of Christ in imitating Him in His kenosis or self-emptying. This imitation or mimesis involves self-emptying, taking on the form of a servant, identifying with others, humility, and obedience. This concept was proposed by Paul in contradistinction to the system of leadership at the time that was centered on accumulating honor, prestige, and position. This type of leadership called for the opposite in laying aside a quest for honor, prestige, and position in the exercise of self-emptying and humility while identifying with others, especially the lowly. The model endorsed by Paul does not call one to serve but to become a servant; in this way, this model is not only about behavior, it is about the ontology of the leader as well.

Leadership is one of the world's oldest preoccupations. The understanding of leadership has figured strongly in the quest for knowledge.
   Bernard M. Bass

CHAPTER 6

THE CONTEMPORARY CONTEXT OF LEADERSHIP

Authentic leadership is a contemporary model for leadership. Authentic leadership development is a process that draws from both positive psychological capacities and a highly developed organizational context that fosters greater self-awareness and self-regulated positive behaviors on the part of leaders and followers producing positive development in both (Gardner & Avolio, 2005). This model conceptualizes leadership as a shared relational process distributed across different organizational levels dependent on collaborative processes distributed and sustained by a network of leaders and followers engaged in collective achievement (Klenke, 2007). This leadership is oriented toward authenticity in the self but also in genuine connections with others in developing effective teamwork and relationships. These leaders are those who: (a) know who they are and what they believe in; (b) are transparent and consistent in their values, ethical reasoning, and actions; (c) focus on positive psychological states such as confidence, optimism, and resilience within themselves and followers; and (d) are known for their integrity (Gardner & Avolio, 2005). This focus on ethics and integrity is important in the contemporary context of leadership issues. In an era of corporate malfeasance and scandals with organizations endeavoring to maximize value at the expense of other objectives like employee well-being and levels of trust, the concept authenticity has intuitive appeal (Klenke, 2007).

Authentic leadership has theoretical roots in the topic of authenticity that has been examined over the years in different disciplines ranging from philosophy, sociology, and clinical and social psychology, and it owes much to modern scholars of identity and self (Gardner & Avolio, 2005). In addition to these theoretical roots, there was a call for a new kind of leadership based in integrity in leadership. Transformational leadership originally saw those like Hitler as transformational leaders, but later changed to view these as not authentic transformational leaders; however, charismatic leadership was still a part of this construct opening a wide range of ethical questions (Ciulla, 2004). When problems surfaced at Enron, Worldcom, and dozens of other companies, the severity of the leadership crisis became painfully apparent, creating a widespread erosion of trust in leaders. As the world becomes more complex, we need truly distinguished leaders with ethically grounded leadership—authentic leadership (George, 2007). In the early 21st century, Luthans and Avolio (2003) began to advance the development of authentic leadership theory. It was advanced by further examination by Gardner and Avolio (2005). It is in this context that authentic leadership, though a new model in leadership studies, is being examined and advanced.

Authenticity is not sincerity or impression management, but it is a self-referential state of being in a commitment to one's values and identity and will positively affect the interpersonal processes that define leadership (Chan, Hannah, & Gardner, 2005). Authenticity is at the core of authentic leadership with a commitment to the reality of self, not for the sake of perception, but for the sake of effective leadership and being true to one's self. Authenticity in leaders operates as a leadership multiplier in that the impact of their leadership is multiplied and this authenticity contributes to higher levels of follower trust which has important implications for outcomes as well (Chan et al., 2005). This type of leadership impacts both leader and follower with positive results in desired outcomes. Authentic leadership is developed over a lifetime of acquiring self-awareness and a commitment to self-regulation and it is manifest through the emergence of authenticity during leadership episodes multiplying effects on performance and outcomes (Chan et al., 2005). This is a life process that impacts one's ability to lead from a continual growth and development in self-understanding and commitment to one's identity and values.

Authentic leadership is defined in large part by evidence of morality in the leadership influence process and this moral leadership is developed through a highly developed self-concept which enables and drives moral agency and virtuous leadership

(Hannah, Lester, & Vogelgesang, 2005). Authentic leadership is moral leadership that produces virtuous leadership in the application of leadership behaviors that proceed from the ontology of the leader. To be authentic, one must know, accept, and remain true to oneself regardless of the environmental contingencies. An important component of this is relational transparency is the commitment of a leader to help a follower see the leader's true self through self-disclosure (Hughes, 2005). Virtuous leadership is developed in the context of being true to self and relational transparency connects the leader and the follower in authenticity. Authentic leaders are individuals who hold true to their fundamental moral character and values, while becoming politically skilled leaders that inspire trust and confidence to incur follower motivation and productive work behavior (Douglas, Ferris, & Perrewe, 2005). Leaders who are high in political skill know precisely what to do in different situations at work and how to do it in a sincere engaging manner (Douglas et al., 2005). Authentic leaders who are skilled at inspiring followers because of their social savvy can become effective in productive outcomes.

Authentic leadership is multifaceted containing elements of self-issues like self-awareness and self-regulation, relational growth, and performance issues. This type of leadership has been examined from several perspectives yielding different but compatible leadership issues for this model. This model of leadership is a values-based model rooted in the ontology of the leader with implications proceeding from the individual for leadership that affects outcomes as well as relational issues. It is a model that impacts both leader and follower in positive ways including issues of trust as well as performance outcomes. Authentic leaders are described as "leading by example" as they demonstrate transparent decision making, confidence, resilience, hope, and consistency between their words and actions, and followers come to identify with these leaders and their values (Gardner, Avolio, Luthans, May, & Walumbwa, 2005). This example of authentic leaders then sets the pace for further authentic leadership development in the organization.

An authentic leader must achieve authenticity through self-awareness and self-acceptance, as well as authentic actions and relationships. These relationships are characterized by openness, guidance toward worthy objectives, and an emphasis on follower development (Michie & Gooty, 2005). This leadership includes not only authenticity in the leader but developing the follower through effective relationships. Authentic followership is an integral component and consequence of authentic leadership producing heightened levels of followers' self-awareness and self-regulation leading to positive follower development and outcomes including higher levels of trust and well-being, making this process an important part of authentic leadership (Mitchie & Gooty, 2005). Authentic leadership begins in the leader but impacts the follower and the organization with positive processes and outcomes.

Self-awareness, unbiased processing, authentic behavior, and relational authenticity intertwine to describe authentic leaders as they behave in daily actions and these actions influence and elevate followers (Ilies, Morgeson, & Nahrgang, 2005). This relational authenticity, when coupled with congruence on values, leads to unconditional trust leading to the free exchange of ideas developing synergistic team relationships which leads to superior performance (Ilies et al., 2005). This authentic leadership is multifaceted affecting not only the leader–follower relationship but directly affecting organizational performance as well. Self-awareness is awareness of one's own personal characteristics, values, feelings, and motives, including the contradictory elements as well leading to one's thoughts, feelings, and actions which has positive implications for leadership well-being and effectiveness while affecting followers' functioning and well-being (Ilies et al., 2005). Authenticity concerning self and in relationships are both part of the authentic leadership model and both have positive effects on leaders and followers, as well as the organization.

Currently, *authentic leaders* are defined as those who are deeply aware of how they think and behave (Cooper, Scandura, & Schriesheim, 2005). These leaders are perceived by others as being aware of their own and others' values, knowledge, and strengths, as well as being aware of the context in which they operate and are confident, resilient, optimistic, and of high moral character (Cooper, et al., 2005). Not only is authentic leadership effective on multiple levels, it also has a multidimensional construct including awareness of self, context, and others, as well as behavioral and ontological characteristics. In addition, authentic leadership may function on several levels such as individual, team, or organizational levels (Avolio et al., 2004).

Klenke (2007) expanded the research to include a component of spirituality using three identity systems (self-identity, leadership identity, spiritual identity) to explore and explain authentic leadership. The concept of self-identity includes self-efficacy and self-liking and assumes that a strong sense of identity is essential to developing authentic leadership (Klenke, 2007). People who are self-efficacious are likely to select and welcome challenging endeavors and to invest the effort and motivation to succeed in those endeavors since they believe they have the ability and resources to execute the specific action (Youssef & Luthans, 2005). The leader identity system consists of leader self-efficacy, leader reputation, and leader prototypicality (Klenke, 2007). Leadership self-efficacy is an individual's perceived ability to perform the functions necessary to regulate group processes in relation to goal achievement (Klenke, 2005). Leader self-efficacy then includes the confidence to regulate and lead a group to a particular goal, not just an individual endeavor.

The spiritual identity system is built upon self-disclosure, self-transcendence, and self-sacrifice (Klenke, 2007). Spiritually authentic leaders draw from the selfless ground of human experience, they recognize the emotional labor involved in leadership and consider sacrifice an integral component of authentic leadership (Klenke, 2005). Fry (2005) proposed that there are four key practices for developing spiritual leadership and by extension authentic leadership: (a) know one's self, (b) honor the beliefs of others, (c) be trusting, and (d) maintain a spiritual practice (prayer, meditation, etc.), which then produce spiritual survival dimensions of calling and membership creating an intrinsic motivating force that elicits cooperative effort among people. There is then a further component of spirituality in the construct of authentic leadership including self-awareness with an aspect of self-transcendence as well.

In Klenke's (2007) model of authentic leadership she includes the cognitive, affective, and cognative elements of the previous theories of authentic leadership while including the spiritual component in her three identity system. The cognitive element includes knowing self, self-efficacy, and moral capacity, while the affective component contains emotional intelligence, optimism, and compassion, with the cognative element containing self-motivation and motivation to lead (Klenke, 2007). This model of authentic leadership adds to existing frameworks by offering a perspective designed to integrate cognitive, affective, cognative, and spiritual components in leadership and followership (Klenke, 2005). In addition, it puts the previous models together in a theory for future research. The uniqueness of this model is its addition of a spiritual component that links authentic behavior to self-transcendence, meaningfulness, and self-sacrifice (Klenke, 2007). This model can be shown graphically as seen in Figure 3.

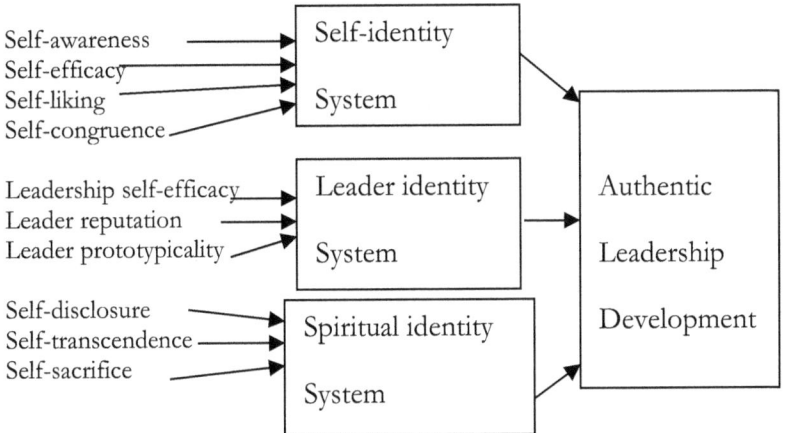

Figure 3. Authentic leadership. Reprinted from "Authentic Leadership: A Self, Leader, and Spiritual Identity Perspective," by K. Klenke, 2007, *International Journal of Leadership Studies*, p. 87. Copyright 2007 by Karin Klenke.

Authentic leadership is a multifaceted model of leadership including elements from at least four areas: cognitive, affective, cognative, and spiritual. The focus of this model is that of self-identity which includes understanding of self and self-efficacy which affects the leader's motive as well as behavior resulting in authentic relationships as well as leadership. This authenticity produces high levels of trust, interaction, and well-being in both leaders and followers. This process produces positive outcomes for leader and follower as well as the organization including higher levels of productivity. The spiritual component includes not only a level of self-disclosure but also that of self-transcendence in moving outside of self. This model of leadership is very broad including not only issues of behavior and attitudes but also that of ontology having to do with the individual as a person.

Authentic leadership is a multifaceted model of leadership that is founded upon the leader developing self-awareness and self-understanding while developing behavior and relational authenticity. This theory has several elements that can be categorized under cognitive, affective, cognative, and spiritual issues. Authentic leadership includes attributes such as optimism, emotional intelligence, and hope. The authentic leader has a positive impact on followers through development of high levels of trust and follower self-efficacy. This positive impact creates a positive influence on the organization as well with higher levels of productivity and on followers by creating a higher sense of well-being in individuals. Authenticity is an issue of the individual—an ontological issue of being—as well as an issue of behavior in the leader and perceptions by the follower. This complex model can be seen in three identity systems of the self-identity system, the leader identity system, and the spiritual identity system.

The approach invites detailed attention to the text itself. Socio-rhetorical criticism integrates the ways people use language with the ways they live in the world.
Vernon K. Robbins

CHAPTER 7

THE EXEGETICAL PROCESS

The research method employed in this examination of 1 Peter rose from the new literary context for New Testament study (Elliot, 2007; McKnight & Malbon, 1994; Witherington, 2007). New Testament literary criticism has recapitulated the classical approaches of literary criticism and has moved beyond New Criticism to deal with the text in terms of the work itself in a move toward overcoming the distinction between theology and biblical studies (McKnight & Malbon, 1994). The church has always maintained that biblical studies and theology belong together, but the two became separated. Until recently, the two have been kept at a distance. Changes are taking place, though, to bring the two back together, among these changes is the New Criticism of literary criticism (Turner & Green, 2000). In literary criticism, the move beyond the interest of the author's creativity and historical reconstruction was a return to the forms of the study of the text, an element of literary study that has been central since Aristotle (Beardslee, 1994). The discovery of literary criticism by biblical scholars is something of an innovation because it involves a self-conscious reading of the Bible in a way that it has not usually been read, and it focuses on the finished form of the text (Powell, 1990). In this is an endeavor to mine the biblical text for theological and practical issues for the understanding of leadership using a research method appropriate to this task. The research method used in this study is sociorhetorical interpretation as described by Robbins (1996). In this examination of qualitative data, the text of 1 Peter was the primary source document.

Though it emerged in the 1970s, socio-rhetorical interpretation received its name in 1984 with an integration of rhetorical, anthropological, and social–psychological insights. Then in the 1990s, the investigation of inner texture, intertexture, social and cultural texture, ideological texture, and sacred texture moved it into an interpretive analytic (Robbins, 2004). Needing a paradigm for research that keeps us in touch with Greek and Greco–Roman literature as well as biblical and Jewish literature, while using an inductive approach to the texts along with insights from ancient and modern treatises on rhetoric, has produced this particular kind of sociorhetorical analysis (Robbins, 1984). *Sociorhetorical criticism* is a textually based method that uses programatic strategies to invite social, cultural, historical, aesthetic, and theological information into a context of minute exegetical activity and this interdisciplinary mode of analysis distinguishes it from other forms of critical analysis (Robbins, 1994). The key to good exegesis and to a more intelligent reading of the text is to learn to read the text carefully and to ask the right questions of the text concerning context and content including literary and historical context (Fee & Stuart, 1993). This minute exegetical activity is the way to understanding these texts for critical analysis.

Reading and understanding texts becomes an active process of producing reality which includes not only the author of the text but also the person for whom they are written and who reads them (Flick, 2002). This production of reality comes through an interpretive framework. Hermeneutics focuses on interpretation and it provides a theoretical framework for interpretive understanding with attention to context and original purpose, especially in the case of legal and biblical texts (Patton, 2002). Socio-rhetorical interpretation is a multidimensional approach to texts guided by a multidimensional hermeneutic; it is an interpretive analytic, an approach that evaluates and reorients its strategies as it engages in a multifaceted dialogue with the texts (Robbins, 2004). Since the examination of 1 Peter in the context of leadership studies has not been done extensively, this method of sociorhetorical interpretation was used to examine the text deeply through this multifaceted interpretive hermeneutic which is important to qualitative research.

The Question for the Process

This study sought to answer the following question: What leadership style and practices are developed by Peter, particularly in 1 Peter, and do these practices and style support or negate other contemporary models of leadership? The purpose of this study was to conduct a multifaceted hermeneutical analysis using a close reading of 1 Peter using detailed exegesis of the text to discover the principles of leadership as taught in this pericope of Christian Scripture..

The method of research was qualitative in mining the text for further understanding concerning leadership in this text as a part of the larger sacred text of the Christian Scriptures. In addition, this research was compared to other qualitative research from a different pericope of the Christian Scriptures since kenotic leadership is a theory derived from the writings of Paul in the text of Philippians. This method of qualitative research was especially important in the understanding of biblical texts (Patton, 2002). This study considered the construct of leadership as developed in the Christian Scriptures and its implications for contemporary leadership. In using socio-rhetorical interpretation, the exegetical process yields data that can be used in developing understanding of principles of leadership from this text and for consideration in contemporary contexts.

In this study, leadership was examined from the inductive study of texts rather than a study of existing leadership. Rather than asking what leadership looks like presently, this study asked the question of what it should look like according to this sacred text of antiquity. Anthropologically, these texts are the material culture of the Christian church. With these texts reality is created by the interaction between author and reader. Because God chose to speak His words through human words in history, every book in the Bible has historical particularity as well as eternal relevance and this tension demands interpretation (Fee & Stuart, 1993). In the Middle Ages, theology was the queen of the sciences or of the domains of knowledge (DeWeese & Moreland, 2005). The sacred text has relevance to this part of history in helping to understand reality in the domains of knowledge, including leadership, and this relevance has been recognized for several centuries.

Socio-rhetorical Interpretation

Socio-rhetorical interpretation began with analysis and interpretation of social and cultural dynamics in texts (Robbins, 2004). Rhetorical interpretation is concerned with strategies that change attitudes and induce action concentrating on techniques of persuasion with an understanding of a wide range of communication strategies both overt and covert (Robbins, 1984). This method focuses on the literary and rhetorical understanding of texts. Literature for years has been aloof from the other studies of the humanities, seeking truth from the interplay between the whole and parts within the text but perhaps literary rhetoric can facilitate the process of interpretation of theology and history (Wire, 2005). This method of interpretation is multifaceted utilizing literary and rhetorical skills in the interpretation of biblical texts.

The New Testament books are fundamentally rhetorical in that their original purpose was to move people to action or conviction yet there were concerns that were behind the texts, therefore, inner textual considerations must be supplemented with treatments of historical settings and impact (Donahue, 1994). It is this interaction and interplay in the text that must be examined for understanding the message of the text. Rhetorical criticism, as embodied in the work of Robbins (1984), integrates literary criticism and social analysis in an approach to uncover the rhetorical strategy and rhetorical situation of a given text (Donahue, 1994). The study of ancient rhetorical conventions may tune the ears of the interpreter to powerful overtones that may not otherwise have been suspected (Turner, 2000). Therefore, this method is uniquely suited for this examination of 1 Peter in an endeavor to discover the leadership principles therein.

Rhetorical criticism is a study of the art of persuasion, and there are several ways that this has been applied to New Testament studies. One, is to study the Greco-Roman rhetoric, and another championed by Robbins looks for modern rhetorical categories in the text (Witherington, 2009a). Other forms include Elliot's (1986) social–scientific criticism and Esler's (1987) study of Luke (Robbins, 1994). However, this study utilized Robbin's (1996) socio-rhetorical interpretation due to its use in doctoral dissertations (Robbins, 2004) and its use of multiple textures of texts for understanding the nuances of the text and the teaching in 1 Peter.

Socio-rhetorical criticism is a form of literary analysis that invites programmatic, self-critical analysis and interpretation of the full range of figures and tropes in the text nurturing disciplined exploration (Robbins, 1994). Socio-rhetorical interpretation is a method which enables the interpreter to bring multiple textures of the text into view with five different aspects of exploring the text. These are: (a) inner texture, (b) intertexture, (c) social and cultural texture; (d) ideological texture, and (e) sacred texture (Robbins, 1996).

Inner Texture

The overall goal of inner textual analysis in socio-rhetorical interpretation is to attain initial insight into the argumentation of the text (Perelman, 1982). The inner texture of a text resides in the features in the language of the text itself, like word repetition, or the use of dialogue; it is the texture of the medium of communication and it is a stage of analysis prior to analysis of meanings (Robbins, 1996). This is an analysis in preparation for interpretation or data gathering for the raw materials of understanding the text. Any strategies of analysis from simple repetition to the most subtle argumentative strategies may contribute to the inner texture of the text (Robbins, 1984). Therefore, in the examination of 1 Peter it was not simply the words that were sought for this texture but also the arguments that Peter developed for his listeners with careful attention to words as well as argumentation development throughout the text. There are six kinds of inner texture in a text: (a) repetitive, (b) progressive, (c) narrational, (d) opening–middle–closing, (e) argumentative, and (f) sensory–aesthetic (Robbins, 1996).

Repetitive inner texture. Repetitive inner texture resides in the recurrence of words and phrases more than once in a unit or pericope occurring in many different kinds of grammatical, syntactical, or topical phenomenon (Robbins, 1996). Sometimes these repetitions occur in topics like suffering or hope (Robbins, 1996). These repetitions are found in 1 Peter in the repetition of the image of shepherd or following the example of Christ or word repetitions like "Him" in 1:8 of 1 Peter.

Progressive inner texture. The next type of inner texture is progressive texture. This texture resides in the sequence of words and phrases throughout the pericope; this emerges out of repetition where words sometimes alternate with one another. Progressive form can be of two kinds: (a) logical progression that advances step by step in sequence or (b) qualitative progression where the presence of one quality prepares for the introduction of another (Burke, 1968). Qualitative progressions occur when an attribute of speech or action, which the reader had no reason to expect, emerges in the characters (Robbins, 1984). A qualitative progression is seen in 1 Peter wherein the hearers are described as newborn babies, then a priesthood, then a chosen race with corresponding characteristics.

Narrational inner texture. The third type of inner texture is narrational texture. Narrational texture resides in voices through which the words in texts speak; the narrator may introduce written texts that speak, or establish a narrational pattern in the discourse (Robbins, 1996). The author introduced texts that speak from the Old Testament in every chapter of 1 Peter. The author also changed the narrational structure of the text in Chapter 5, moving from general instruction to a focus that is first-person communication.

Opening–middle–closing inner texture. The fourth type of inner texture is opening–middle–closing. This texture resides in the nature of the beginning, body, and conclusion of a section of discourse, repetition, progression, and narration regularly work together to create this form (Robbins, 1996). This is seen in the text of 1 Peter in his discussion of submitting to authority in the opening in Chapter 2 Verse 13, then in the middle is a discussion of following the example of Christ in Chapter 2 Verse 21, then the closing is a further discussion of submission to authority in Chapter 3 Verse 1, ending with a summary in Chapter 3 Verse 8. This kind of texture may be complex due to variations that occur with different kinds of openings, middles, or closings (Robbins, 1996).

Argumentative inner texture. The fifth type of inner texture is argumentative form. This texture investigates multiple kinds of inner reasoning in the discourse; it could be logical with assertions and supporting clarifications or qualitative with images that encourage the reader to accept the portrayal (Robbins, 1996). Rhetorically, 1 Peter can be seen as a rhetoric containing five arguments that are interrelated ending with the exhortation to leaders. In addition, there are several smaller logical arguments in the body of the document such as: (a) major premise, abstain from things that make war on the soul; (b) minor premise, fleshly desires do this; (c) conclusion, keep away from fleshly desires as found in Chapter 2 of 1 Peter (Witherington, 2007b).

Sensory–aesthetic inner texture. The sixth type of texture of inner texture is the sensory–aesthetic pattern. This texture resides prominently in the range of the senses the text evokes or embodies, like thought, emotion, sight, sound, or touch; initial insights may come from identifying different types of literature like a proverb or a parable (Robbins, 1996). In Chapter 4 of 1 Peter, during a discussion of suffering, the text embodies several emotions that would be in opposition to the natural emotions of suffering, such as rejoice, not surprised, and not ashamed. This sensory–aesthetic texture may give color and tone to other textures in the discourse (Robbins, 1996) as is the case in the argument of dealing with suffering being punctuated with joyful emotions rather than remorse.

Intertexture

Intertexture is the interaction of the language of the text with outside material and physical objects like historical events, texts, customs, values, roles, institutions, and systems, with a major goal of ascertaining the result of processes of configuration and reconfiguration of phenomena in the world outside the text (Robbins, 1996). It is clearly seen in 1 Peter that Peter reconfigured the concept of suffering with rejoicing. Sometimes this texture inverts a tradition, turning the rhetoric of a previous tradition on its head to create a new dramatic tradition (Robbins, 1996) as is the case with connecting suffering and rejoicing in this pericope. In addition, Peter interacted with the language of the Old Testament of shepherd as a leader to configure the idea of leadership for the church. According to Robbins (1996), there are four categories of intertexture: (a) oral–scribal, (b) cultural, (c) social, and (d) historical.

Oral–scribal intertexture. Oral–scribal intertexture involves a text's use of any other outside of itself including inscriptions, Greek poetry, or the Hebrew Scriptures (Robbins, 1996). There are several ways that the text can use these words from other texts. Recitation is transmission of speech from oral or written tradition in the exact words or with some omissions (Robbins, 1996). Peter mentioned that chapter 2 verse 6 comes from Scripture and then quoted from the Hebrew Scriptures.

Recontextualization presents wording from the biblical texts without explicit statements or implication that the words were written anywhere else (Robbins, 1996). In 1 Peter 4:18, the author quoted from Proverbs 11 from the Hebrew Scriptures with no mention or implication of its source in the other text. Reconfiguration is recounting a situation in a manner that makes the later event new and this new event replaces or outshines the previous event (Robbins, 1996). In 1 Peter, the cornerstone in Zion is reconfigured as the Chief Cornerstone which is Christ the cornerstone of the new race of believers.

Narrative amplification is an extended composition containing recitation, recontextualization, and reconfiguration (Robbins, 1996). In 1 Peter 2:21-25, there is a narrative amplification concerning the suffering of Christ wherein there is a recitation in verse 22 and a reconfiguration in verse 24 with the story of the suffering servant from Isaiah recontextualized in the suffering of Christ for sins. Thematic elaboration is when a theme emerges as a thesis near the beginning of a pericope and meanings of this theme unfold throughout the text, using rationale, opposites, analogy, example, and testimony (Robbins, 1996). This is seen in 1 Peter as the theme of submission and authority unfolds throughout the text with the example of Christ, the analogy of the shepherd, and the testimony of Peter.

Cultural intertexture. Texts have an interactive relation to cultures of various kinds and cultural intertexture appears in words, concept patterns, or configurations that are known only to the particular people inside the culture (Robbins, 1996). In 1 Peter, the picture of shepherd and sheep, though not explained, is an insider understanding based in the culture of Israel from the Hebrew Scriptures in Jeremiah 23 concerning shepherds not as leading natural sheep, but leading people. Cultural intertexture appears in a text through: (a) reference, a word or phrase that points to a person or tradition known to people through; (b) allusion, a statement that presupposes a tradition exists; or (c) an echo, which is a subtle indirect reference that evokes a concept of the cultural tradition (Robbins). This example in 1 Peter is a reference.

Social intertexture. Social knowledge is commonly held by all persons of a region no matter their cultural location; generally it is visible from observing behavior and objects (Robbins, 1996). In 1 Peter, it is the common understanding of the roles of master and slave in their social relationships and that which is part of the normal household code. This social knowledge comes generally in one of four categories: (a) social role, (b) social institution, (c) social code, or (d) social relationship (Robbins, 1996).

Historical intertexture. Historical intertexture concerns events that have occurred at specific times in specific locations looking for corroborating evidence of the events as stated in the text (Robbins, 1996). One of the issues in the examination of 1 Peter is the period of the suffering that is discussed in the text. Was it a later persecution or an earlier persecution? Was it general difficulties faced by the believers or was it threats of death from a powerful emperor? These are the issues of historical intertexture.

<u>Social and cultural texture</u>

Analysis of the social and cultural texture takes the interpreter into sociological and anthropological theory addressing the issue of the social and cultural nature of the text searching out the kind of person that lives in the world of a particular text (Robbins, 1996). These social and cultural phenomena are primary topics in rhetorical theory (Robbins, 1994). The social and cultural texture of a text raise questions about the response to the world and the cultural alliances and conflicts evoked by the text (Fowler, 1986). This texture of the text emerges in specific social topics, common social and cultural topics, and final cultural categories (Robbins, 1996).

Specific social topics. Texts with a substantive religious texture contain certain ways of talking about the world as seen in Wilson's (1969) typology of sects, and each kind of response creates a kind of culture that gives, meanings, values, and actions to people (Robbins, 1996). These responses/views of the world can be seen in Table 5.

Table 5: Social Response as a Type of Social Rhetoric

Response	Views the world as
Conversionsist	Corrupt: if people can be changed then the world can be changed
Revolutionist	Only the destruction of the world, natural and social order will suffice to save people
Introversionist	Irredeemably evil: salvation can be obtained only by the fullest possible withdrawal
Gnostic (manipulationist)	Needing transformed relationships: salvation is possible if people learn the right means to address problems

Thaumaturgical	Needing special dispensations with a focus on the concerns of individual people for relief for present, specific ills
Reformist	People creating an environment of salvation by using supernaturally given insights to change the present social organization into a system that functions toward good ends
Utopian	In need of a new social system in which evil is absent, people must take an active role in replacing the system

Note. Reprinted from "Socio-Rhetorical Criticism: Mary, Elizabeth, and the Magnificat as a Test Case," by V. K. Robbins, in *The New Literary Criticism and the New Testament* (pp. 185-186), by E. McKnight & E. Malbon (Eds.), 1994, Valley Forge, PA: Trinity Press. Copyright 1994 by V.K. Robbins.

Most historical manifestations of religious communities exhibit a relationship of two or three of these responses to the world (Robbins, 1994). In the text of 1 Peter is found the thaumaturgic response with the focus on the present suffering and the gnostic response of transformed methods of coping with suffering by rejoicing. This Gnostic response is also seen in the leadership issues in 1 Peter in transformed methods in leading others in ways that are counterintuitive in following the example of Christ.

Common social and cultural topics. Everyone living in an area knows the common social and cultural topics; this is the overall environment for the specific social topics in the text (Robbins, 1996). There are several social and cultural topics where a distinction needs to be drawn between present western culture and first-century modes of behavior and understanding (Robbins). An important issue for the study of 1 Peter is honor, guilt, and rights culture, particularly in relationship to the issue of authority which impacts leadership. The young men that were written to in this text were probably tempted to seek to make their own way in the Greco–Roman world and to establish their honor and honor claims in public (Witherington, 2007b). The context of 1 Peter is set in a society of honor and shame, which would have caused the example of Christ in leading to be countercultural as well as counterintuitive.

Final cultural categories. Final cultural categories of rhetoric are those topics that most decisively identify one's cultural location, which concerns the manner in which people present their propositions and arguments (Robbins, 1996). These appear in different culture rhetoric: (a) dominant culture rhetoric, (b) subculture rhetoric, (c) counterculture rhetoric, (d) contraculture rhetoric, or (e) liminal rhetoric (Robbins). In 1 Peter is found counterculture rhetoric wherein the writer responds to the dominant culture. Counter culture rhetoric evokes a new future and it implies alternative minicultures that make provisions for both sexes and a wide range of age groups capable of influencing people over an entire lifespan and develop appropriate institutions to sustain the group (Roberts, 1978). It is this rhetoric that is seen in making specific provisions for leadership that follow the example of Christ and understand the new perspective on suffering.

Ideological Texture

Ideology is an integrated system of beliefs, assumptions, and values, not necessarily true or false that reflects the needs or interests of a group (Davis, 1975). The primary subject of ideological analysis is people; the issue is the social cultural and individual location of writers and readers concerning particular biases, opinions, and preferences of a particular writer and reader (Robbins, 1996). The first operation is for the readers to find their location in the specific social topics and the final cultural categories of the previous section, and then the function would be to look at one's relation to groups and examine one's mode of discourse as an interpreter (Robbins, 1996). The area that was particularly relevant in examining 1 Peter was mode of interpretation for discourse since the method that was chosen was socio-rhetorical interpretation; however, this study also examined commentary from those of other ideologies in commentary such as historical–critical discourse, other forms of socio-rhetorical interpretation, rhetorical criticism, and social-scientific criticism. This type of dialogue broadens the discussion of leadership and deepens the discoveries as they are done in the context of community—a community of commentators.

In addition, there are spheres of ideology that can be examined and in doing so the discussion moves to texts and examining them in three ways: (a) analyzing the social and cultural location of the implied author, (b) analyzing the ideology of power in the discourse, and (c) analyzing the ideology in the mode of intellectual discourse in the text (Robbins, 1996). In 1 Peter and its relationship to leadership a major issue for the text is that of power. In 1 Peter, those in power were persecuting the believers and yet the response was one of rejoicing and submission, not of resistance. Peter also addressed those in power directly as masters, husbands, and elders with instructions in the proper use of power patterned after Christ.

Sacred Texture

Sacred texture is examining the text for insights into the nature of the relation between people and the divine, locating the ways that the text speaks about God or gods and talks about realms of religious life (Robbins, 1996). The text in this study had an abundance of issues for sacred texture examination like God being seen as Father and Christ who is at God's right hand in heaven. In addition, there were many issues of religious life in living as holy and as a priesthood of believers as well as being called to follow the example of Christ in suffering and in leadership. Sacred texture can be examined under several important and relevant issues particularly in studying: (a) deity, (b) a holy person, (c) a spirit being, (d) divine history or eschatology, (e) human redemption, (f) human commitment, (g) religious community, and (h) ethics (Robbins, 1996). The text of 1 Peter contains issues in each of these eight areas for sacred texture. Of importance for this study was the study of Christ as a holy person—even deity in the text—who provided for human redemption, who set the example for the religious community to follow in multiple levels calling for human commitment in suffering and in leading while being an important part of the divine history of the text.

Socio-rhetorical interpretation is a way into the text for understanding and interpretation that is thick and rich with meaning. In this way of interpreting, there are five main categories in developing the texture or the understanding of the texture of a text. This method has developed since the 1970s from literary criticism, rhetorical criticism, and anthropological studies. Socio-rhetorical interpretation began to emerge after 1975 with a goal of integrating rhetorical and anthropological modes of interpretation as well as integrating sociological–psychological insights (Robbins, 2004).

Socio-rhetorical interpretation is a multidimensional approach to texts guided by a multidimensional hermeneutic engaging in multifaceted dialogue for an interpretive analytic (Robbins, 2004).

Each of the five research areas of texture also have several subcategories which are then further subdivided. In the setting of this research, there were many questions that could be asked for research in the text as the text took on many dimensions in imitation of life which has many layers and dimensions. Life is not one dimensional and neither are texts, this method allows, even presses for, a full examination of the text for it to give its full expression for life. This multidimensional approach can be seen graphically in Table 6.

Table 6: Textures in Socio-rhetorical Interpretation

Inner texture	Intertexture	Social–cultural texture	Ideological texture	Sacred texture
Repetitive	Oral–scribal Recitation Recontextualization Reconfiguration Narrative Amplification Thematic	Specific topics Conversionist Revolutionist Introversionist Gnostic–manipulationist Thaumaturgic Reformist Utopian	Individual locations	Deity
Progressive	Cultural Reference Allusion Echo	Common topics Honor/shame Individualist–dyadic Contracts Challenge–response Exchange systems Peasants Limited goods Purity codes	Relation to groups Clique Gang Action set Faction Corporate group Historic tradition Multiple traditions	Holy person
Narrational	Social	Final categories Dominant culture Subculture Counterculture Contraculture Liminal culture	Modes of intellectual discourse Historical critical Social–scientific Postmodern Sociorhetorical	Spirit being
Opening–middle–closing	Historical	Spheres of ideology Implied author Location Power		Human redemption

Argumentative				Human commitment
Sensory–aesthetic Emotion-fused thought Self-expressive speech Purposeful action				Religious community

Note. Reprinted from *Beginnings and Developments in Socio-Rhetorical Interpretation* (p. 17), by V. K. Robbins, 2004, Atlanta, GA: Emory University. Copyright 2004 by V. K. Robbins.

Since the end of the first century Christian authors such as Clement of Rome and Bishop Polycarp of Smyrna were inspired by its (1 Peter) words of consolation, exhortation and hope.
   John H. Elliot

CHAPTER 8

THE TEXT OF 1 PETER

Peter was the most important of the disciples of Jesus, with one foot in the ministry of Jesus and one foot in the early church, bridging and linking the two (Witherington, 2007). First Peter did indeed derive from Simon Bar Jonah, a fisherman until he became a follower of Jesus; this document merits close scrutiny as it provides a clear link with the original founder of the Jesus movement—Jesus Himself—and Peter becomes the great bridge figure between Jesus and the early church (Witherington, 2009a). Other than Jesus Himself, Peter, humanly speaking, most shaped the movement known as early Christianity in conjunction with the apostle Paul (Witherington, 2007). This text is an important aspect of the thinking, teaching, and theology of the early church that formed the ministry of the church and is relevant today in parsing out truth for application in the contemporary context for life and leadership. These were important issues to the early church and in the texts of the early church as well as in the present human context.

Some authors or commentators see the central theme of the writing of 1 Peter, or the reason that Peter wrote this document, was to show the appropriate Christian response to suffering to those who were under some form of persecution and undergoing suffering (Green, 2007; Jobes, 2005; Marshall, 1991; Seagraves, 2010). Clearly, it was in this context that 1 Peter was being written. Yet, the text addressed multiple issues both practical and theological to teach the believers how to live in this hostile cultural environment. Often missed in the sociological study of 1 Peter is the fact that the author was constructing a rhetorical world—a world of advice and consent, of persuasion and dissuasion, where certain beliefs and behaviors were inculcated not merely for social reasons but also for theological reasons

(Witherington, 2007). This is an ad hoc pastoral document where the theological discussion undergirds the values, virtues, and practices that are inculcated by the author and this is the only New Testament document that addressed the issue of Christians being resident aliens within the macrostructures of larger society (Witherington, 2009b). These theological underpinnings for practical issues in the context of society include issues of authority and leadership in both ideological and practical ways. The practical issues of daily living are supported by the theology of this rhetorical document that endeavors to convince the hearers to live counter-intuitively and counter-culturally in areas like suffering and leadership. These areas need to be explored for the nuances of truth and reality in this pericope through examination of the textures of this text in connection to leadership and authority.

The traditional thinking is that 1 Peter followed the norms of letter writing of the time (Clowney, 1988; Jobe, 2005; Marshall, 1991). However, Witherington (2007) challenged this notion by declaring that much of the document's form and structure cannot be accounted for through epistolary analysis or letter writing norms of the day, instead it was structured on the basis of rhetorical conventions meant to be read aloud to various audiences. If this document was meant for oral and rhetorical communication, it must then be interpreted in line with its intent. In viewing the beginning of this document, it is found that it is more than a pro forma opening or greeting, it dives headfirst into the deep waters of the discussion of God's election (Witherington, 2009b). First Peter is a rhetorical document that needs rhetorical norms for understanding and interpretation.

A rhetorical outline has been proposed by Witherington (2007), with a *proposito* of living according to the hope you have been given then proceeding through five arguments ending with a *peroratio* of humility and self-control in suffering. This outline highlights the call to the hearers of this text to live in a certain way as instructed by the author. The author was constructing a rhetorical world of advice encouraging certain behaviors and beliefs based upon theological underpinnings as developed in the text (Witherington, 2009b). In the midst of these exhortations is an encouragement to a certain kind of leadership following the example of Christ as lived out in a hostile world and cultural context.

Socio-rhetorical critics are interested in the nature of texts; they approach a text much like an anthropologist "reads" a village, perceiving texts to be thickly textured with simultaneously interacting networks of signification. They interpret and reinterpret texts as forms of activity between writers, readers and audiences (Robbins, 1994). These interacting networks provide a thick texture of understanding in the text yielding a nuanced and profound understanding of the text tied to the intent and understanding of the author. These texts were written to be read and heard therefore this reality must be considered in this texture of the text. Rhetoric meant public speaking or oratory, which for centuries even in literate cultures remained the paradigm of all discourse, including that of writing, but writing enhanced rhetoric by making it possible to study the rhetoric after delivery (Ong, 2002). Therefore, this rhetoric of 1 Peter can be examined for its textured meaning and advice since it was written down not only for reading but now it can be studied as well.

This thick texturing and interacting networks of signification will not yield neat linear categories such as is the custom in the 21st century. Therefore, the text was divided into several pericopes for examination from different rhetorical perspectives that were useful and relevant for that particular section in connection to leadership issues in this text. Every pericope did not necessarily contain the same rhetorical framework even though all of them did fit within the robust framework of Robbins (1996) socio-rhetorical interpretation. Once the sections of the text were examined, then the macrostructure of the text was examined within the same rhetorical framework. In each section there were discussions of the ramifications of the discoveries in that pericope of text for leadership.

Peter, an apostle of Jesus Christ, to those who reside as aliens.
Peter, NASB

CHAPTER 9

I PETER – PERICOPE 1

1 Peter 1:1-12

This section of verses 1- 2 of Chapter 1 is seen as an epistolary prescript by commentators (Campbell, 1998; Davids, 1990; Grudem, 1999; Witherington, 2007). However, in this study, it was examined together with the section that ends with Verse 12. This section of 1:3-1:12 is considered by some to be an opening thanksgiving (Davids, 1990; Marshall, 1991). However, others viewed this as an *exordium* in rhetoric (Campbell, 1998; Green, 2007; Witherington, 2007). The purpose of the *exordium* is to create a good atmosphere to prepare the audience to receive the instruction that follows (Green, 2007). Characteristic of an *exordum*, this pericope contains no explicit exhortations or commands but attempts to create an atmosphere for Peter's argument by describing the life of his readers in the most ideal terms to put them at ease and as a form of encouragement to follow his subsequent exhortations (Jobes, 2005). There are several textures of interpretation available in the beginning of introduction to this instruction from Peter to the churches and those in the churches. Peter introduced himself as an apostle, which has ramifications for the church and those in the church. This concept of apostle in consideration of cultural intertexture is a concept known by those in the culture of the church. It reiterates the word apostle that was used by Jesus in calling those disciples who were to be with Him in ministry in Mark 3:14, designating them as apostles. These were the same 12 apostles, including Peter, in the early church after the resurrection of the Lord in Acts 1. By identifying himself as an apostle, Peter gave his credentials and authority to write to the people of God conveying the promises and commands of God to the people (Marshall, 1991). The word *apostle* means "to send," and in the New Testament, was one sent by Christ or His church for some specific task (Witherington, 2007). Peter stood on the ground of authority given to him as a leader in the church to write and instruct or persuade the people. These twelve apostles took leadership roles in the transition period in the early parts of the book of Acts having responsibilities for activities of the church and for choosing leaders (Witherington, 2007). In Spencer's (2008) phenomenological study of Peter's apostolic leadership, he concluded that his leadership was energized by the Holy Spirit and was linked to the extension of God's purposes. He described God's plan to others while consciously influencing others to adopt the same vision God had given him. He assumed the responsibility to act on behalf of God. In the context of the culture of the church, apostles were seen as leaders with authority in the church and to speak to the people of the church to give insights for theology and practical living and impart a vision of God's plan as seen in 1 Peter. In Acts, this is seen through their preaching and in the epistles such as 1 Peter this is seen through the rhetorical writing to the people who were followers of Jesus.

Though Peter was mentioned as the apostle and the leader or author, the focus quickly changed to sacred texture and a repetitive inner texture. In this short pericope, God is mentioned three times, the Father two times, Jesus Christ six times, and the Spirit three times. Significantly, these repetitions are grouped together in an opening–middle–closing format of inner texture as well. God the Father and Jesus are the focus of the opening section in Verses 1-3, with discussions of theological issues of election, sanctification, and foreknowledge. The next section begins with a declaration of the resurrection of Jesus Christ from the dead. Resurrection referred above all to the divine inauguration of a new world order marking the divine establishment of divine justice and marks the vindication of the righteous who have suffered unjustly according to the contemporary Jewish Literature (Green, 2007). In this way, the intertexture of this verse in 1 Peter is connected not only to the facts of salvation history but also to the literature of the time signifying the initiation of a new time.

The middle section of the inner texture from Verses 3-10 centers around Jesus and the believer, with a focus on words such as salvation, suffering, glory, and rejoice. There are also several times that the pronoun "Him" is used in rapid succession referring to Jesus Christ and the believer's relationship to Him. In

Verse 8, the focus is that even though the person has not seen Jesus, that the person loves, believes, and rejoices in Him. This new world order is a world that is connected to Jesus Christ connecting the invisible world to the visible through the resurrection of Jesus Christ. The result is salvation of one's soul. But this new world reconfigures reality, defining physical realities in new ways. This is the intertexture of reconfiguration. The concept of suffering would be familiar to the hearers of this epistle, but to rejoice is a new concept for this new world order. In Hebrew literature, it was understood that suffering was the result of evil and the opposition of God as seen in Job 4:8-9, "Those who plow evil and those who sow trouble reap it, by the breath of God they are destroyed." Even Jesus' disciples endorsed this way of thinking when they asked in John 9:2, "Who sinned, this man or his parents that he was born blind?" Of course, Jesus said neither, understanding the nature of suffering, but the people around Him did not. Peter now took the long feared concept of suffering and reconfigured it. Now it was not the result of evil and to be feared as a judgment from God, it was part of the process of refining faith and a place of rejoicing. Peter gave a fuller explanation of the divine purposes behind the grief which were occasions when God refined and purified the faith of His people and genuine faith emerged from these trials, which was of great value (Grudem, 1999).

Peter drew the hearers into solidarity with the people of the Old Testament by providing a basis for this identity speaking of them as chosen and later explaining how Israel's' prophets were moved by the Spirit of Christ (Jobes, 2005). This solidarity helped them see the progression to being the new chosen people with a reconfigured rhetorical world of mercy instead of judgment; of heaven being the focal point rather than an earthly city and of individual salvation that affects the person, not national status. These were resident aliens and the solution was not a return to Jerusalem, it was something powerful yet internal, operated by faith and transformation. This is seen in the reconfiguration of suffering as no longer judgment with little or no relief, instead it is a part of the process of change.

The final section or the closing for this inner texture is found in Verses 11-12 with a focus on the Holy Spirit and the believer. It was the Spirit working in the prophets that spoke of this new time coming through the sufferings of Christ and now this present work of the gospel is to the believer. The believer is in this new time and age that has been initiated by the sufferings, the resurrection, and the glory of Christ. Glory is a manifestation of God's excellent power or as an excellent reputation of honor; it is a state characterized by honor, power, and a remarkable appearance (Friberg & Friberg, 2000). In one sense, the glory speaks of the power of God, and in another sense, it speaks of a reputation of honor and power when speaking of people.

Power is an issue of ideological texture (Robbins, 1996). What are the issues of power here in the text? In this section, God revealed His power through giving salvation and through the suffering of Christ. God revealed Himself as powerful in mercy toward humans. However, there is no sense of power on the human level in this section who are called resident aliens. They are recipients of God's merciful power, who are active in responding to God's power properly in the midst of suffering by rejoicing and knowing there to be good results from this way of living.

In the midst of the opening–middle–closing texture, there is also a progressive texture which begins in Verse 4 with an imperishable inheritance reserved, then in Verse 5, this salvation is ready to be revealed. In Verse 6, there is rejoicing over this, then in Verse 7, the result is praise glory and honor, then finally the revelation of Jesus Christ is the culmination. The person moves from having an inheritance for them, and then it moves to revelation, with results of praise then the culmination of the revelation of Jesus Christ, obtaining or walking in salvation in Verse 9. This progression moves from the theological base of salvation reserved, through the revealing and rejoicing in the person with a revelation of Jesus, a life full of joy and glory. Peter said his readers may have to experience grief in trials so that their faith can redound to praise glory and honor, but he did not say whether this praise is the praise God gives to His people on the last day or the praise which people give to God; it seems more likely that it is the praise that God gives to His people (Grudem, 1999). This praise and honor then is that which results from a life lived in faith and though this may be future, but in Verse 8 it speaks of the present rejoicing and glory. This salvation brings the person not only to a life of joy, but full of glory of reputation, honor, and power. Power does begin to show itself here, but not as a means to a purpose but as the result of a changed life. These different textures of inner textures can be combined and seen graphically in Table 7.

The issues for leadership in this section proceed from two important aspects of this beginning pericope. In this introductory section, Peter established the theological foundation upon which the rest of the text was built. This foundation is that God as revealed in the Father, His Son Jesus Christ, and the Spirit uses His power through mercy to bring salvation to people. This is power from God and power in humans comes from a progressive process of obtaining the outcome of faith living out the inheritance in joy and glory. Secondly, suffering is reconfigured from the result of evil and divine judgment to the process of refining the faith that is necessary for a life of joy and glory. God is the foundation of all including power and salvation. This salvation and even power comes to humans through God's mercy as seen in the resurrection of Jesus Christ and as this salvation is progressively lived through suffering and response to God the person is transformed.

Table 7: Inner Texture of 1 Peter 1:1-1:12

Verse	Repetitive texture	Opening–middle–closing	Progressive texture
1	Jesus	1:1-3 God Father Jesus	
2	God, Father, Jesus, Spirit		
3	God, Father, Jesus	1:3-10 Jesus and you	
4	You, heaven		Reserved
5	God, power (salvation)		Revealed
6	You, rejoice, suffering		Rejoice
7	Jesus, glory		Result, revelation
8	Him (4x), you (3x), rejoice, glory		Joy and glory
9	Salvation		Salvation of soul
10	You, salvation		
11	Suffering, glory, Spirit	1:11-12 Spirit and you	
12	Spirit, heaven, you (3x)		

Additionally, leadership is seen in Peter sending this document as an apostle of the Lord, one sent on a mission. This form of leadership was linked to the extension of God's plan through instruction and vision given to the people of God. The apostles in the culture of the church were seen as leaders with responsibility and authority to give direction and influence the church as well as to appoint other leaders. The apostolic leader was energized by the work of the Holy Spirit; it is an internal work that displays in the leader influencing others for kingdom purposes.

1 Peter 1:13-16

This short pericope is included in the next section by some commentators (Campbell, 1998; Green, 2007; Marshall, 1991), but Witherington (2007) set it apart as a separate section as a *proposito* for the rhetoric to follow in the rest of the document. The function of the proposition was to make a smooth transition from what had gone before and to set up the thesis for what was coming. This section draws a conclusion based on the previous verses using the word "therefore" and sets up the theme of holiness while believers remain strangers in a strange land (Witherington, 2007). "Therefore" (*dio*) relates this section to the former one, which is the basis of the commands in these verses, in that the reception of salvation must issue in a life of holiness, reverence, and love (Blum, 1981). Clearly, this conjunction indicates that Verse 13 is a pause implying that the argument from the preceding verses is now rounded off and applied to the situation of the readers and it introduces the next section (Jobes, 2005). With Verse 13, Peter moved from describing the new perspective held by those who have been reborn to an exhortation to a new way of life with a new perspective (Green, 2007).

In this short section there is a repetitive, progressive, and open–middle–closing inner texture. In addition, there is an intertexture recitation and reconfiguration in this proposition that sets the tone and agenda for the following rhetorical arguments. The progressive texture is seen in three progressive statements in Verse 13. The grammatical structure of the whole verse suggests a sequence of events (Grudem, 1999). The progression moves from prepare, to keep, to fix; this is a progression along a continuum toward putting one's hope on the future revelation of Jesus Christ. The main emphasis of Verse 13 is putting one's hope wholly in the eschatological consummation of the grace of

God in Jesus Christ (Blum, 1981). It begins with prepare minds for action. This is literally "gird up your loins" and refers to the practice of tucking garments around the waist to be free for action and the mind here is the center of understanding (Marshall, 1991). Peter likely meant that they should prepare themselves for some heavy and serious thinking (Witherington, 2007). The mind, however, is not to be understood narrowly as only intellectual life but as that which determines conduct as well (Jobes, 2005). This preparation of the mind includes clear understanding, but to the point of affecting behavior as well, it is an internal issue that impacts external conduct.

The second part of the progression is to keep sober. The first step is to prepare, now the second is to keep. When this word is used in the context of thinking, it refers to a broad range of sobriety, namely restraint and moderation, which avoids excess in passion, rashness, or confusion, hence self-control (Jobes, 2005). In the New Testament, this word is used figuratively of being free of every form of mental excess and confusion (Friberg & Friberg, 2000). The mind and thoughts must be prepared for action but then it must be kept sober without confusion, especially in the new context of salvation that is personal and where suffering is for progress rather than judgment. This again is an internal issue.

The final piece of the progression is the ultimate step in fixing hope on the grace to be brought at the revelation of Jesus Christ. This aspect connects the present to the future. Setting hope is present but hope is future-oriented and it is set on something to be brought in the future—the full revelation of Jesus Christ. This term for *hope* in the New Testament refers to an expectation which is much stronger than a vague sense of wishing; it does not imply absolute certainty but it does imply a sense of confident expectation, strong enough for one to act on the basis of it (Grudem, 1999). Peter anticipated that hope would be displayed in a changed life and believers were urged to set their hope completely on the coming grace (Green, 2007). Moreover, they were to set their hope fully on this coming grace with an undivided confidence and to place no confidence in the things that society trains us to put our hope in such as status or money (Jobes, 2005). Such hope in great blessings when Christ returns prompts a reordering of priorities according to God's agenda (Grudem, 1999). The exhortation is to order one's life in the present in light of the future full revelation of Jesus Christ and the ramifications of that truth for the believer.

The object of this progression is the grace that comes from the revelation of Jesus Christ. Note the present tense in the phrase "the grace being brought to you"; the implication is they already have grace in part and it is coming in the revelation of Jesus Christ. In this, Peter expressed the tension between the present and future aspects of salvation (Witherington, 2007). There is a present preparation and living that is affected by the future full revelation of Jesus Christ. This should change one's behavior, but it begins internally in the mind, soul, and will of the person. This progression begins with the inner person in preparing the mind, and in keeping sober both internal issues of the mind, then of setting hope an issue of the will. These are focused on the object of the revelation of Jesus Christ. Together these should affect how one lives; this is ontological. Every aspect of this progression, which is a pivotal verse in this document, is ontological.

The opening–middle–closing texture begins in Verse 13 and goes through Verse 16. The first section in Verse 13 is an exhortation about the present based in the future. Then Verse 14 changes focus to the past and finally Verses 15-16 are an exhortation about the present. The beginning and middle form a foundation for the exhortation in the closing. In addition, the first two sections speak of internal issues like mind and lusts, whereas the closing speaks of holiness as an internal ontological issue of being holy followed by an exhortation concerning behavior.

The exhortations in Verse 13 are about the present life of the believer, but based in the hope of the future revelation of Jesus Christ. The main emphasis of Verse 13 is on putting one's hope wholly in the eschatological consummation of the grace of God in Jesus Christ; now we have a beginning of that grace but the consummation of that grace comes at the full revelation of Jesus Christ to come (Blum, 1981). This setting of hope is in the present but based on the future and it relates to issues of the inner person.

The middle section speaks about the past life of a believer. This verse calls believers not to conform themselves to their previous desires, referring to sinful cravings, in the sense of the root cause related to sin (Witherington, 2007). Notice this is a call to not conform to the sinful desires, not to the sinful behavior. Sinful desires are the root. This is an exhortation having to do with being first before behavior; it is ontological. This ignorance Peter referred to was not an ignorance of a general knowledge of God but was linked to sin and evil desires (Witherington, 2007). It was a lack of understanding coupled with desires that bring disobedience. The term "lust" is rooted in the Jewish concept of the evil impulse in humans and the problem is that the goods of this age become the goals one seeks rather than means to the goal of serving God (Davids, 1990). The issue is an internal issue from the past that must not be revived in one's life.

Then the closing of this section is found in Verses 15-16 with the exhortation to present holiness. It returns to the present and is the point of the texture. Living in the present in light of the future and no longer living in the past is so that one can be holy in the present. It is here that the repetitive inner texture is found as well with the word "holy" found four times in this one verse. This particular pericope is pregnant with meaning. It is the place of the end of the beginning–middle–ending texture, as well as the location of the repetitive texture as well as a place of recitation and reconfiguration in intertexture.

The example of the Holy one is put forth as the standard. But the call is to be holy first like the one who called. This is an issue of being of ontology; then behavior proceeds from that source of holiness. The root meaning of holy is to be separated out for something or someone, this is separation to God rather than separation from the world, but this means separation from sin since God and sin have no common meeting point (Witherington, 2007). This calling is a calling to God and therefore a separation from the way of life of the world and this call is a call to imitate God (Davids, 1990). Peter then quoted from Leviticus 19:2 to reinforce his point of holiness that it was from one's connection to God. Peter quoted Leviticus 19:2 exactly as found in the LXX where the customs and rituals of the priests are found, however, Peter did not mandate this holiness code for his first-century readers (Jobes, 2005). Holiness is an issue of the inner person first in preparing the mind and fixing hope while rejecting past desires and imitating God Himself in holiness of character. This holiness will work out or manifest in holy behavior or behavior that shows one separated to God.

This exact repeating of the Leviticus 19:2 in 1 Peter is a recitation from the Old Testament. Peter's application of the Old Testament was exact but differentiated to establish that Christians should be set apart from their surrounding culture in a way that is consistent with God as revealed in Jesus Christ (Jobes, 2005). This recitation connects Israel of the Old Covenant with these believers in Jesus Christ. As Israel was the elect and called people in the Old Testament, so now Christians are the called people of the new age—called to God and a new way of life (Davids, 1990). However, this concept of holiness undergoes a reconfiguration at this point since holiness in the Old Testament was a concept of codes, commands, and regulations, it changes in the present context. Peter's differentiated application of Leviticus preserved the authority of God's word to Israel as binding on Christians but it did not prescribe the Levitical code as the way to be followed (Jobes, 2005). Holiness as seen in 1 Peter is an ontological issue formed through issues like hope and understanding, while leaving the ignorance of evil desires. This produces behavior that shows one is set apart to God, but it is not ritual or command driven. Holiness is reconfigured to be the imitation of God in character rather than an external set of rules. Holiness still affects behavior, but as a result of ontology not as the result of command. To be holy as God is holy includes a pervading holiness that reaches to every aspect of personality not only in avoiding outward sin but also in maintaining a distinctive delight in God (Grudem, 1991). Holiness begins within in imitation of God in internal areas which manifest outwardly, not in ritual, but in ways that delight God. The fundamental idea of holiness is that of a position or relationship existing between God and some person and it includes the ethical holiness of God that is separation from evil and sin (Berkhof, 1996). Holiness is a communicable attribute of God or attributes that are shared with humans; His holiness provides the pattern for people to imitate and individuals, as well as the church, must grow in holiness (Grudem, 1994). The holiness of God was revealed perfectly in Jesus Christ and is revealed in the church as the body of Christ (Berkhof, 1996). Contextually, this exhortation to holiness was made to those who had been born again and internally had placed their mind and hope on the revelation of Jesus Christ. This exhortation was made not based upon regulations but upon relationship. Those separated to God and who had set their hope properly should be holy and this should affect their behavior. Several of these textures can be seen in Table 8.

Table 8: Inner Texture of 1 Peter 1:13-16.

Verse	Progressive	Opening–middle–closing	Repetitive
1:13	Prepare minds		
1:13	Keep sober		
1:13	Fix hope		
1:13	On revelation	Present future	
1:14		Past	
1:15		Present	Holy (2x)
1:16		Present	Holy (2x)

In this pericope are several issues for leadership. This short section is the proposition for the rest of the document setting the foundational ideas that are relevant in further discussions concerning the issues of leadership. The message is that the believers must prepare themselves to be able to receive and live the exhortations to follow. The preparation is internal, involving the mind, the will, and the very being of the individual. In addition, this preparation involves being holy in imitation of God. These are issues of ontology and mimesis or imitation.

As Peter exhorted the believers concerning authority and leadership, the foundation of it was an ontological change that had taken place in the person. This change was an imitation of God in His being holy.

This ontological change affected behavior, but it was internally motivated. Peter reconfigured a recitation from the Old Testament wherein the people were exhorted to holiness, but in that context it had to do with ritual and regulation. In the new context of the writing of Peter, it was based upon relationship with God through the revelation of Jesus Christ and one setting their mind, hope, and will on this revelation.

Holiness then is reconfigured from external to internal. Then Peter had reconfigured two issues in this new age after the resurrection, that of suffering and that of holiness.

You also as living stones, are being built up as a spiritual house for a holy priesthood to offer up spiritual sacrifices acceptable to God through Jesus Christ.
   Peter, NASB

CHAPTER 10

I PETER – PERICOPE 2

<u>1 Peter 1:17-2:10</u>
This is the first argument in Peter's rhetorical presentation. It involves both theology and ethics with the latter grounded in the former in that the saving work of Christ both for and in the believer is the ground of Christian ethics (Witherington, 2007). It is seen in the first two sections and this one as well that the exhortations to behavior are grounded in the internal work of salvation; the work inside the being of the person. In this longer pericope, there are several textures; progressive, open–middle–closing, and repetitive along with intertexture recitation, recontextualization, and reconfiguration along with cultural intertexture. In addition, this section begins with thick sacred texture.

The sacred texture of this pericope gives three vivid pictures concerning human redemption. The three pictures are that of blood, milk, and stone, which are also connected to an opening–middle–closing texture that is seen as well. The first picture is considered in the past tense, having already been redeemed with the blood of Christ. This picture not only refers to the past actions of the person becoming a believer, it also refers to the past action of Christ not only shedding His blood but also Him being foreknown before the foundation of the world. This is a picture with a long history. Peter inscribed the sacrificial death of Jesus into the timeless plan of God and expanded on what is already known to his audience, building on the premise of Christ's preexistence showing that God's own agenda stood behind Jesus' redemptive work and the plan to redeem individual people (Green, 2007). This plan was revealed in part in the Old Covenant that Peter referred to here. The idea of redemption by the blood of the lamb is clearly rooted in the Old Testament most frequently found in the books of Leviticus, Psalms, Exodus, and Isaiah; it is related to the Old Testament concept of deliverance from foreign exile and being delivered from sin that characterized their former way of life (Jobes, 2005). The imagery is that of the Passover lamb which was closely connected to redemption from Egypt and the readers' "Egypt" may have been cultural and not physical (Davids, 1990). Peter did not connect redemption directly with freedom from sin and guilt, nor did he portray redemption in contrast to the current society, but it is defined as being in contrast to the way the readers lived before they came to faith in Christ though culturally venerated Peter described as useless (Jobes, 2005). This redemption was the beginning point for a new way of life for the believers—a new birth. New birth into the one true reality established by the resurrection of Christ showing a contrast between the futility of a misperceived reality and the true reality now found in Christ (Jobes, 2005). The reference to blood indicates that Christ's was not just an ordinary death but rather a sacrificial death and the language suggests that Peter had the lamb sacrificed in Passover in mind and by New Testament times this sacrifice had come to be regarded as a means of atonement for sin (Marshall, 1991). Peter took an issue of the Old Testament having to do with redemption and deliverance in the Exodus and reconfigured it in the context of the sacrifice of Christ for deliverance from the past life and redemption for sin that is applied now to the believer in Christ.

The second picture having to do with human redemption is that of milk; it has to do with growth in respect to salvation. This is a commonly used metaphor for religious teaching, which causes growth; growth in spiritual stature, though contextually, Peter identified nourishment with the Lord rather than with His word or teaching about Him, but Peter's aim is to encourage his readers toward spiritual growth (Marshall, 1991). In human redemption there is not only a new birth but also growth as a spiritual person that is important. Peter used this metaphor of milk to instruct them to crave the things of God as babies crave milk, but the word describing this milk is best understood as reasonable in the sense of being true to ultimate reality, in that life in this new reality requires sustenance that is true to ultimate reality of the new creation as established in the resurrection of Jesus Christ (Jobes, 2005). There is a new reality and one must grow in this new reality in understanding and living in it. The more-of-the-Lord-to-be-had by the believers involves putting off all evil and deceit and to not do so would stunt spiritual growth (Jobes, 2005). Spiritual growth was an important aspect for the believer and it came through knowing the Lord and receiving His teaching resulting in transformation in life.

The third picture is that of a living stone. This is a picture of building with believers as living stones and Christ as the Chief Cornerstone to become a spiritual house with the new identity of the chosen race. Though heavily indebted to the Hebrew Scriptures and interpretive traditions of Judaism, Peter transposed them in light of the new reality inaugurated by Christ's resurrection in affirming the believers as living stones in relationship with Christ the Living Stone resulting in the new identity of believers as a chosen race and royal priesthood (Jobes, 2005). The redemptive picture moves from a growth analogy to a purpose analogy to become a spiritual house—a new identity related to Christ. Peter switched rapidly from the metaphor of spiritual nourishment to that of coming to Him and Christ is the chosen stone instead of the rejected stone upon which a spiritual house is built—a place of family and the presence of God (Marshall, 1991). This house is built by the living stones of maturing believers, forming the identity and purpose of the believers. He is building up believers into a spiritual house which is a structure characterized and filled by God's Spirit; it is clear that the author viewed the Christian community as the new temple of God, where God dwells (Witherington, 2007). Again Peter used Old Testament Scriptures to reconfigure a familiar concept in a new way: the temple is no longer a geographic building but a people coming together as a spiritual building for God's presence. The concept of the nonphysical church replacing the material temple in Jerusalem is widespread in Christian writings; the house of God is no longer to be thought of as a physical building but a living house where God lives (Davids, 1990). This picture of human redemption gives three analogies to help form the understanding of the elect as the community and the purpose of that community. The community of the elect is to become the new chosen race and a spiritual house wherein is the presence of God. But why? The purpose is to grow spiritually to be able to be built into a spiritual house, in this is not only purpose but identity as well. But why is this important?

First, it is significant to notice the different textures in this section of Scripture. There is an opening–middle–closing texture that begins with a birth concept of new birth and discussion of the blood of redemption. Then the middle in Chapter 2 speaks of growth in salvation—of becoming—using the analogy of milk for growth and the living stones in becoming a living spiritual house. Finally, in the ending, it describes who the believers become in Verses 9-10 as people of God's own possession.

This is further reinforced by the progressive texture in these verses moving from birth to babies, to living stones and the spiritual house, ultimately becoming the royal priesthood, the chosen race, the holy nation, and God's people. All of these pictures or progressions lead to the culmination of what the believers become found in the repetitive texture at the conclusion of this pericope: the people and the priesthood of God. The concept of the rejected stone as the Chief Cornerstone is reconfigured as a spiritual house with a people that are chosen and holy and a priesthood that is holy and royal. The image of the living stones being built into a house whose cornerstone is Christ speaks of unity, significance, and purpose of all believers and this church is not primarily a social organization but the new temple where the transformed lives of believers are offered as sacrifice to the glory of God (Jobes, 2007). The purpose of the house is to bring glory to God on the earth. The way this happens is through the people of God being priests unto God.

Peter's task was not to read the Scriptures Christologically but to show how a Christological reading of the Scriptures guided the church in the formation of identity and mission (Green, 2007). This guidance showed the purpose of the believers in forming the house for the glory of God through a process of spiritual birth, growth, and becoming—becoming the priesthood and the people of God. As part of the holy priesthood, all believers are to have a function in that community, as together they are God's house or temple and their job is to offer up themselves to God as spiritual sacrifices (Witherington, 2007). Peter recontextualized the text in Exodus 19:6 concerning the priesthood and the nation as spoken to Israel and now directed it toward the church as the new priesthood. Alluding to the narrative of God's deliverance of His people from bondage in

Egypt, Peter borrowed language from Exodus 19:6 with an emphasis on the priestly identity of God's people as the community of believers in the world (Green, 2007). The royal priesthood means that they are a priesthood and they belong to a king, indicating they serve the in-breaking kingdom whose king is Christ and the purpose of their special position is that they might announce the glorious deeds of God (Davids, 1990). They are a kingdom of priests whose function or purpose is to bring glory to God on the earth as the spiritual house or living stones in much the same way that Christ the Living Stone and Chief Cornerstone brought glory to God. The believer functions as priest by offering spiritual sacrifice of self to God and advancing the rule of God on the earth by living in proclaiming the presence of the real God in this new reality after the resurrection of Jesus Christ from the dead. The intention here is that Christians are to publish abroad the works of God in creation, redemption, and the revelation of Jesus Christ; this heraldic praise is their reason for existing (Davids, 1990).

The repetitive structure includes a repetition in Verses 9-10 of the believers being the people of God; His own possession. The chosen race or chosen people are reconceived from an Old Testament text to refine the identity of the audience of Peter (Green, 2007). He reconfigured the Old Testament context into his present setting declaring the believers to be the new people of God. This is a process of change from birth to growth to building to become; it is a process of ontological change. It is not only a change in being, but with that change it is also a change in purpose and direction. The new *ontos* is the people and priesthood of God, the new purpose is to show forth the praises of God, and the new mission to advance the rule of the kingdom of God on the earth. The responsibility that accrues to the community is to announce the wondrous acts of the one who called people out of darkness to declare His praise that is vertical (worship) and horizontal (proclamation) of the acts of God, especially the saving death of Jesus Christ and God having raised Him from the dead (Green, 2007). Peter concluded the thought with a double reference to the change that had been wrought in the lives of his readers involving their external status as well as their internal personal experience and at one time they were "no people" but now they were "God's people" (Hiebert, 1992). The action of the believers as priestly community is to offer spiritual sacrifices acceptable to God and it expresses the immediacy of the community's relation to God (Ellliot, 2000). They had been changed to become the people of God both in their status in relationship to God as well as in their being in who they have become as the holy (set apart), royal (kingdom) priesthood. The different textures of this pericope can be seen in Table 9.

Table 9: Inner Texture of 1 Peter 1:17-2:10

Vs.	Progressive	Opening–middle–closing	Repetitive
1:23	Birth	1:17-1:25 Blood—redeemed	
2:2	Babies		
2:5	Living stones	2:1-2:8 Grow in salvation Become (milk, stone, house)	
2:5	Spiritual house		
2:5	Holy priesthood		Priesthood
2:9	Chosen race		People (2x)
2:9	Royal priesthood		Priesthood
2:9	Holy nation		
2:9	God's people		
2:10		2:9-10 Who you are	People (2x)

Witherington (2007) insisted that this concept of priesthood does not imply a special class of leaders or priests in the church. Power (1998) contended that as vocational priests fulfill their priestly duties they serve as leaders setting examples for other believers to fulfill their priestly duties. However, we do not find a basis in Verse 5 or 9 for the Reformation doctrine of the priesthood of all believers in that Peter's emphasis was not on the role of the individual as a priest but on the priestly identity of God's people and the role of the community (Green, 2007). What is the role or the connection of leadership in this issue? Is priesthood a concept for leadership? Directly, no, but indirectly, yes.

Peter, in this text, was writing as a leader and an apostle. Peter identified himself as an apostle and this expression can be taken as a confirmation that Peter accepted and willingly engaged in the role he had been given as leader. For him, mature leadership involved giving clear instructions for living and specifying behaviors that were important to extend the authority of God (Spencer, 2008). As the community of priests of those elect members of God's household, they needed leadership that Peter was providing. He was constructing reality for this community of priests. It did not mean priest or priesthood, but community of priests; he spoke to the believing community as community not as individuals (Elliot, 2000). He came to them as an apostle to the set apart community to lead them. Peter's goal was the redefining of the reader's self-identity and to show them what was true—to point to the ultimate reality in light of the new reality of the resurrection (Jobes, 2005). It is also seen in these early pericopes that Peter reconfigured suffering, holiness, redemption, and even priesthood. Priesthood was reconfigured from a separate group of people to the community in agreement with Exodus 19, though this was not the practice under the Old Covenant. Peter also came to the community of priests or the household of faith to help them grow—to move from birth to becoming to being, In becoming this household or priesthood, they offered spiritual sacrifices. This change process was internal ontological instead of external or law-driven as in past thinking. This type of leadership was ontological in two senses. One, it had to do with growth and change in one's being. Two, it had to do with revealing and understanding ultimate reality.

1 Peter 2:11-3:12

First Peter 2:11-3:12 is the second argument in Peter's rhetorical construction. We have arrived at the heart of the argumentation where Peter was especially concerned about the two important subjects of submission to authority and suffering, but with a focus on submitting to authority (Witherington, 2007). This section is about honorable conduct as a subordinate in civil and domestic realms, focusing on honorable behavior of the household of God in the larger society. The mood changes from indicative to imperative, from affirmation to delineations of responsibilities in society (Elliot, 2000). "I urge you" for the first time makes Peter's appeal personal and it also reflects Peter's tender attitude. He did not command them, but appealed to them as one walking alongside of them; he appealed to their own sense of right (Hiebert, 1992). This section about suffering and submission to authority is both personal, yet direct, and a call to action-based upon the previous indications of who they were as the people of God. True holiness was not procured by the application of external authority but by awakening and strengthening the personal desire of those individuals (Hiebert, 1992). Peter was appealing to them to learn to live in the world in a particular way. He emphasized the status that believers have as the people of God—chosen by Him and in fellowship with Him to prepare them for lowly service. Since they were God's royal people, they could be servants following the example of Jesus. This whole section is a direct antithesis of the world where everyone demands their rights (Clowney, 1988). This section takes a new direction exhorting the believers to live out their new life in surprising ways in relationship to suffering and to authority.

In this pericope, there are several pertinent textures to examine. In the inner texture of this section are found a thick repetitive texture as well as a chiastic structure, which is similar to an opening–middle–ending texture. In addition, there is an argumentative inner texture in this pericope. There are several aspects of intertexture found as well, including a cultural intertexture issue as well as a social intertexture issue, and a narrative amplification that includes both recitation and recontextualization. There are several issues of power found in the ideological texture. A social–cultural texture is found as well concerning the culture of the recipients of this document. Finally, there is a sacred texture seen in this section concerning both human redemption and a holy person. This extended section is tied together with these thick textures as well as a common argument that is woven through the exhortation.

This section is full of repetitions in the inner texture. These repetitions are sometimes contrasting concepts such as evil or evil doers as contrasted with do right or doing what is right. In this section, Peter encouraged active resistance in the face of trials by doing good or what is right and he sketched that which constitutes good behavior in contrast to evildoing (Green, 2007).Other repetitive words include *submit* or *submitting* and *suffer* or *suffering* and *God*. The underlying theme in this cycle of exhortations is the need for a spirit of submissiveness on the part of believers and they were urged to glorify God in the context of a hostile world through good conduct (Hiebert, 1992). This good conduct involved submission to authority even when it was oppressive and suffering but not as a result of evil. In this whole section, the general principle of submission is developed concerning submission that is due every human being in their different roles and in submission to suffering, not as inevitable but as the Lord's calling (Clowney, 1988). Submission is a key theme and is linked with doing good; in fact, the purpose of those in authority is to punish those who do evil. Submission to authority, doing good, and suffering are connected in contradistinction to doing evil. Although this material speaks of suffering, it also contains a fair degree of optimism about what their good conduct can accomplish, but it is mostly in connection to God's grace not human nature (Witherington, 2009b). Suffering can lead to glory and a testimony for the Lord but submission does not necessarily lead to relief of human suffering, though it can help provide insight for new paradigms for life and leadership.

As with the rest of the document, this section is heavily theocentric, with many repetitions of *God* ensuring that all of life is structured in relation to God, His will, His perspective, and His glory (Green, 2007). The suffering and the submission are considered in the context of relationship to God and giving glory to God. The way of life endorsed for Peter's readers was that of a sustained good lifestyle in the midst of difficult situations where they would be witnesses bringing unbelievers into the community of Christ so that they could glorify God as well (Jobes, 2005). This good lifestyle and response to suffering is ultimately theocentric leading to others glorifying God who come from the outside into the Christian community.

Submit to authority usually means obedience, but it is excepted when commanded to sin and this is the Christian's responsibility toward all forms of rightful human authority whether one is in agreement or not (Grudem, 1999). This concept includes not just spiritual authority but includes human authority even among the unbelievers. Submission is not a derogatory concept of forced submission, but a voluntary acceptance of a position of obedience to a superior authority; not cringing as weaklings but free acceptance of the duty of submission which is motivated by loyalty to the Lord (Hiebert,

1992). This submission then is a proper response to authority and it is a voluntary response not a forced or enforced one upon others. In Verse 13 is the first of several instances of the verb *to submit* that is a term of thematic significance throughout 1 Peter and it presumes a concept of natural and social order prevalent throughout the Greco-Roman world. It denotes recognition of and respect for authority and order involving subjection to superiors, namely God and humans in position of authority;it acknowledges one's subordinate position (Elliot, 2000). This position of submission helps to define one's relationship to authority, not grasping for authority but recognizing and living in the context of order.

In this setting, the argumentative texture of inner texture is also found. Argument in this discourse begins with a strong warning against fleshly desires which sets the rhetorical tone of the rest of the argument: the major premise is to abstain from things that war against the soul; the minor premise is that fleshly desires do this; and the conclusion is to keep away from fleshly desires (Witherington, 2007). Reasoning may be described as qualitative when the descriptions and images encourages the reader to accept the portrayal as true, through analogies, examples, and citations of ancient testimony (Robbins, 1996). The argument we are considering here in 1 Peter stresses that the audience is to continue to do good works as a witness to their faith, where the imperative is followed by confirmation and example (Witherington, 2007). The confirmations are found in the exhortations to submission and the example is found in Christ who suffered for sin. Then the imperative is to follow the example of Christ (Witherington, 2007). Following the example of Christ is the point and the solution for the believer in living in society and to be able to win the war waged against the soul. The argument begins with urging the believers to win the war against the soul, the inner person, and ends with the solution of following the lead of the overseer of their souls. This is an issue of the soul, not just of the punishment of evildoers. Soul is used to denote the inner moral nature—the seat of self-conscious human life, man's inner being (Hiebert, 1992). In referring to soul, the author is referring to the inner person or the inner life of the person (Witherington, 2007). The issue is an internal issue of soul or one's inner being.

Lastly, inner texture in this pericope includes a special opening–middle–closing texture. This particular texture has a chiastic structure with two sections leading up to the middle and two sections rescinding from the middle with a focus on the middle section. The outline of the chiastic structure can be seen in Figure 2. This chiastic structure begins with instructions to everyone and then to slaves concerning submission to authority. It's followed with the example of Christ as the middle or the pivot of the chiasm, followed by instruction to wives and then instruction to everyone (Green, 2007). The presence of a passage about Christ's suffering is unexpected in a discussion about slaves, wives, and husbands, yet here Peter joined ethics to theology in a profoundly convincing way (Jobes, 2005). The theology about the Messiah and what He has done in redemption becomes the example for believers to follow in their life in the context of the culture of the world. In this structure, Peter focused on Christ as the example in areas of suffering, submission, and authority. Jesus is the key to winning the war of the soul as seen in the previous paragraph, but He is also seen as the key to understanding submission and authority. He ultimately suffered under authority, yet submitted to that authority and, ironically, by doing so He became the authority of the Bishop and Overseer of souls.

In the intertexture of this section is found a cultural intertexture from the writings and thinking of the Old Testament. This is the concept of shepherd. The cultural picture of shepherd is used in connection with Jesus as the suffering servant who becomes the Shepherd leader. The title shepherd is suggested for the suffering servant in Isaiah 53:6. David used the image of shepherd to describe God's care for His people and the image of sufferer and shepherd are brought together again in Zechariah (Clowney, 1988). The concept of straying sheep was used of Israel only when she was without a leader or under wicked rulers. The picture of God as Shepherd in known in the Old Testament and it took on messianic overtones in some passages and, in parts of the Jesus tradition, He is explicitly called shepherd (Davids, 1990). Many were called shepherds, kings, princes, priests, prophets, and elders in the era of the Old Testament were generally called shepherds (Conner, 1989). Leaders in the cultural tradition of Israel were called shepherds while this title was also applied to God and to the Messiah and finally to Jesus. In this context, this describes the leadership of Jesus.

In this same section of 1 Peter 2:21-25, there is a narrative amplification containing a recontextualization of the Old Testament from Isaiah 53 but then moves on to expand into a reconfiguration of the suffering servant from Isaiah reconfigured as Jesus the suffering servant Messiah. This is a creative use of Old Testament material where elements of Christ's passion are interwoven with phrases and allusions of Isaiah 53 moving beyond an appeal to what is written to an explanation of its significance (Jobes, 2005). This explanation amplifies the existing text into the understanding of Jesus as that servant connecting the past to the present of Peter's readers, but then he connected it with their future telling them to follow His example. The resurrection of Jesus Christ is not only a historical event it is also a hermeneutical one allowing new understandings of the Old Testament writings (Jobes, 2005). The primary concern of this text is really not about Christological reflection, but he deployed Christology in service of instruction about Christian life and ecclesiology wherein the believers were called to lives patterned on the obedience of Christ (Green, 2007). This explanation integrates the text of the suffering servant in Isaiah with work of Jesus Christ showing the significance of Christ both in redemption and for an example for the believers to follow in suffering and His leadership as shepherd. Peter was challenging a pervasive view of reality that an individual's lot in life is traceable to deeds done whether good or evil and it is believed to be enforced by God (Green, 2007). Nevertheless, in showing that God will rescue the righteous through suffering and that the suffering servant is the consequence of others' sins, he is restructuring the life-view of his readers (Green, 2007). Peter defined reality for his readers based upon a reconfiguration of an important text continuing to redefine suffering.

In this reconfiguration, the believer is exhorted to follow the example or in the steps of Jesus Christ. This material drawn from Isaiah's portrait of the suffering servant is used to show Christ as God's suffering servant as an example and an enabler for behavior of the believer (Elliot, 2000). The theme of imitating Christ is common in the New Testament and in the Hellenistic world, but the word in this passage is not simply of an example, it is to copy like school children must carefully trace the pattern of letters to learn to write (Davids, 1990). Mixing metaphors, Peter added the image of following in footsteps and both pictures underlie the importance of Christlike performance and the dispositions of Christ shown in the life of Christ in one's life (Green, 2007). The Greek word translated *example* is a powerful image suggesting the closest of copies and that this model is not one of many but this is the one model—this is a strong image associating the Christian life with the life of Christ (Jobes, 2005). The believer is to follow the example of Christ closely and specifically in suffering, in attitude, and as the new shepherd of the soul. The concept of sheep following after the shepherd—in his footsteps—gives the image of walking in Jesus' footsteps which is the Shepherd's path of safety and deliverance (Jobes, 2005). The essence of good education in antiquity was following good models, imitating them (Witherington, 2009b). This imitation of Christ was the way of the new hermeneutical reality after the resurrection in imitating the shepherd.

In the social intertexture of this section the instruction to those with different roles in society were widely recognized on some level in society. Peter developed significant points of contact with the household code known throughout the Greco-Roman world characterized by their focus on obligations of submission, however these codes were "baptized" by Peter adapting them to the demands of faith commitments with certain innovations (Green, 2007). These domestic roles had been influenced by a long standing Greco-Roman tradition of instruction concerning appropriate behavior in connection to the civil and domestic spheres of life and these two spheres formed the building blocks of society dating back as far as Plato (Elliot, 2000). In "baptizing" these Greco-Roman traditions, Peter was not afraid to adapt them into his teaching concerning submission and order and he was able to innovate into the context of the faith commitments of the believing community.

In the social and cultural texture of this document is found that the context of this writing is in a culture of honor, guilt, and shame. In this section is found the use of honor language. Peter wanted the readers to establish their honor in public not by engaging in honor challenges but rather by doing the good for others (Witherington, 2007). It was the structure of social order that established the context for the outworking of honor and shame in this society wherein honorable behavior was to live in accord with one's social status and to behave shamefully was to withhold respect to superiors (Elliot, 2007). This helps set the context of the connection to doing good and submission to authority. Those written to in this text were probably tempted to seek to make their own way and to establish their own honor and honor claims in public (Witherington, 2007). Nevertheless, Peter's exhortation was to develop a way of life that was full of submission rather than seeking their personal honor.

The ideological texture of power is seen here. Though the believers were exhorted to submit to authority there was a difference between the uses of power by those in authority. The purpose of the civil government was to punish those who do evil with the connotation of making the wrongdoer pay for the wrong done and to praise those who do right as a reward for good conduct (Grudem, 1999). This reward and punishment system in government was the way of authority or use of power in the social order. Nevertheless, another way of authority is proposed in the life of Jesus Christ in contradistinction to this way of authority or power application. Peter referred to Jesus as the Shepherd and Overseer of their whole being; a shepherd by feeding and caring for them and an overseer as one who watched over a city or individual. These two pictures show the benevolent care of God from both a Jewish and a pagan background (Davids, 1990). Peter suggested that turning from sin included turning to Christ and submitting to His leadership as Shepherd and Overseer (Grudem, 1999). Jesus is the leader of their inner true selves and as Shepherd and Overseer he not only leads, feeds, and sustains, He also guides, directs, and protects them (Hiebert, 1992). This use of power is counter-cultural in the context of Peter's readers whose leaders legitimately used power for punishment and reward. It was nowhere implied that this use of power was improper. However, submission to the authority of Jesus as leader had a different power context. Instead of a system of punishment and rewards, it was a system of care and guidance.

There is another contrast here in the difference between free men and bondslaves. Peter declared his readers to be free people, but free to choose to be slaves of God. It was not an escape from service but a change of masters, and Jesus as the suffering servant was the example to be followed (Jobes, 2005). Freedom is for service, not in the sense of self-determination, but freedom from the former empty way of life to divine service; submission is an expression of freedom not coercion (Green, 2007). The contrast is counterintuitive in that the result of true freedom is voluntary submission to God and those in authority. The path to freedom is following the example of the suffering servant and the impetus for freedom is not self-determination but service.

Human redemption is central to the discussion in this pericope as part of its sacred texture. The believer is to return to the Bishop and Overseer of the soul and in this way is able to effectively follow the steps of the Lord; He bore sins so the believer could live to righteousness. Verse 24 stated the effects of Christ's suffering and crucifixion: the transfer of human sins upon Him and the liberation of the believer from the compulsion to do what is wrong and empowerment to live justly (Elliot, 2000). Christ bore in His body punishment for sins of others, a substitutionary atonement so that humans can experience redemption and live to righteousness (Witherington, 2009b). Peter's point in the verse was that when people are converted they come under Jesus' care in that Christ the suffering servant takes away the sins of the readers and as Shepherd He now cares for them in their needs; it is the message of a new life and the possibility of forgiveness (Marshall, 1991). Human redemption is provided by Jesus Christ as a substitute for sins but this conversion carries with it a change—a new life to live to righteousness.

In the context of sacred texture, there is also a special person that is held out as an example in regard to submission to authority. The person is Sarah and it is in the context of the extended section of the wives submitting to their husbands. Peter presented Sarah as a paradigm of submission because she called her husband "lord" and because of her obedience, particularly when Sarah obeys Abraham in deceiving Pharaoh in Genesis 12 thereby showing Sarah's Christlike decision where she was willing to suffer to save her husband's life (Jobes, 2005). In this story, Abraham deceived Pharaoh by denying that Sarah was his wife. Sarah agreed, but it endangered her while it protected Abraham. In this, Peter provided a role model of a virtuous woman from Israel's tradition, replacing Greek role models and subtly subverted Greco-Roman culture (Jobes, 2005). The protomatriarch Sarah was cited as a specific instance of subordinate and honorable behavior and though she was one of the holy wives of old, was introduced in Verses 5-6 as a support to the earlier thoughts of wives submitting to their husbands (Elliot, 2000). This way of submission modeled by Sarah is important for two reasons:(a) in speaking to a new and difficult situation in the culture and (b) in describing how a person develops this kind of submission.

Peter shared the universal view of the subordinate status of wives but his rationale was decidedly Christian in content and without parallel in the New Testament (Elliot, 2000). In Greco-Roman society, it was expected that wives would have no friends of her own and worship the gods of her husband, but this would cause trouble in the case of an unbelieving husband with the believing wife worshipping a different God than her husband. Peter instructed her to submit to her own husband's wishes, not that of society (Jobes, 2005) Peter's directive was not to countermand her faith, it was how to live in this situation—not to worship the gods of her husband—and this was a nonconformist position (Green, 2007). Her directive was not to cease to worship the Lord, but to work it out with submission to her husband in mind. The writings of Greek philosophers did not usually address women as Peter did here and this direct instruction to wives implies that they had a measure of moral responsibility and choice which was unprecedented in Greek thought. The submission of the wife was no longer motivated by Roman society, but by the example of Christ. Peter both upheld and subverted the social order (Jobes, 2005). His instruction took on a distinct Christian character with Christ as the center instead of society and in this allowed for the transformation of society.

In addition, submission is seen here as developed internally by developing the hidden person of the heart. This inner person can be developed and reveals a contrast between inward and outward beauty. Character—not appearance—is what matters to God, so develop beauty in the inner person of the heart which refers to one's disposition, frame of mind, and way of relating to and dealing with the outer world. This is a positive character trait that is described as imperishable (Witherington, 2007). To the external adornment of the body is contrasted the internal moral adornment of a person's heart, denoting the inner self considered to be the organ of thought, disposition, and intention (Elliot, 2000). It is the internal character that must be adorned to enable one to love a life of true submission even in the face of suffering and opposition. This spirit is the fruit of the Spirit in the heart and is not distinctively feminine even Jesus described Himself as gentle (Clowney, 1988). Peaceful and gentle are the character of the human spirit or the human spirit as influenced by God's grace and such a spirit is a cloak of virtue that can be worn or not and this is in opposition to restless, rebellious, disturbed, and insubordinate (Davids, 1990). This internal character is an issue for men and women, it is valuable to God, and it is an imperishable quality that can be put on as a cloak or developed in the inner person. Part of the texture of this pericope from 1 Peter can be seen in Table 10.

Table 10: Inner Texture of 1 Peter 2:11-3:12

Verse	Repetitive	Opening–middle–closing
2:11	Soul	
2:12	Good deeds, evildoers, God	
2:13	Submit	A. Instruction for everyone 13-17
2:14	Evildoers, do right (good)	
2:15	God, do right (good)	
2:16	Evil	
2:17	God	
2:18	Submit, good	B. Instruction for slaves 18-20
2:19	Suffering, God	
2:20	Suffer, God, do right	
2:21	Suffer	C. Example of Christ 21-25
2:22		
2:23	Suffering, righteously	
2:24	Righteousness	
2:25	Souls	
3:1	Submissive	B' Instruction for wives 3:1-7
3:4	God	
3:5	Submissive	
3:8		A' Instruction for everyone 3:8-12
3:9	Evil (2x)	
3:10	Evil	
3:11	Evil, do good	
3:12	Evil, righteous	

Concerning issues of leadership in this passage, the concepts of suffering and submission are prominent with the idea of not grasping for authority. In suffering, one is to follow the example of Christ, who is held up as the leader, as the overseer, and shepherd. This shepherd leadership is one of care, as well as leading by example from ontological issues that impact behavior. This is the second exhortation to the imitation of Christ and this aspect means a very close following. Christ leads by setting the example, being an overseer who guides and a shepherd who cares for the followers. This example to be followed includes suffering and leading. In this context, submission is seen to be an issue of the inner person with an exhortation to put on or develop inner character issues. In development as a person, it is seen that the inner man can and should be changed to develop an imperishable inner quality. Peter, as a leader, continued to define reality for the readers and reconfigured authority by contrasting godly authority as caring and guiding with worldly authority that is reward and punishment-driven. He also gave direction that could transform society, but relationally, not with radical shifts. Included in this transformation and new definition of reality is using freedom to serve. The suffering servant becomes the ultimate leader and then sets the example or the model not only for life, but for leadership as well, for others to follow very closely.

For you have been called for this purpose, since Christ also suffered for you, leaving you an example for you to follow in His steps.
  Peter, NASB

CHAPTER 11

I PETER – PERICOPE 3

<u>1 Peter 3:13-4:11</u>
This is the third argument in Peter's rhetorical construction. In this pericope, Peter showed that trials which come from unbelievers cannot harm those who live according to virtue. This argument builds on what has come before, especially concerning suffering (Witherington, 2007). Peter dug deeper into this countercultural reconfiguration of suffering for the believer continuing to use the example of Christ as the hermeneutical lens for understanding. The problem of suffering despite doing right has already been addressed but now it becomes the subject of sustained attention and it draws out the moral and social implications of sharing in the sufferings of Christ (Elliot, 2000). The thought of suffering for the faith has hovered in the background but now it becomes the central theme wherein Peter wrote to encourage, strengthen, enlighten, and comfort his readers so they would stand firm in the midst of suffering and to prepare them for what was ahead (Hiebert, 1992). They not only needed resolve to face the trials but they also needed to understand the place of suffering in the life of faith, as well as how to live in the midst of this tribulation and moving ahead in their faith. At the end of his argument, Peter applied an eschatological sanction, in that since the end is near it is more important to do a better job in imitating Christ (Witherington, 2007). This argument used rationale from both the past in the sufferings of Christ and the future—the end of all things to encourage the believers in the present. Peter set all of life in an eschatological horizon that finds its basis in the redemptive sufferings of Christ; in the pattern of the sufferings of Christ that believers should live accordingly as ones who will come safely through the present to judgment at the end (Green, 2007). Believers are not only redeemed by the suffering of Christ, they

are shown a pattern of life as well that has eschatological ramifications. Peter counseled his audience in their suffering tied to the previous instructions to slaves and wives, all of these words were directed to a Christian audience whose status in the world was similar to that of slaves and wives in Roman households wherein every attitude encouraged of believing wives is now encouraged among followers of Christ in a pagan society (Green, 2007). These exhortations were to all believers, not just to certain subgroups, and Peter used the common understanding of household codes to paint the picture of effective Christian life and service as explained more fully in this section of his argument. Christ is the example here of suffering but in this section His final victory and authority over all powers provide a basis for encouragement and believers are to put behind them the old way of life that is contrary to the purposes of God (Jobes, 2005). The argument moves from the new concept of suffering to a new concept of living in light of eschatological reality.

In this pericope, there is an extensive inner texture with repetitive texture, and two opening–middle–closing textures. This pericope moves through a time element as well in a progressive texture beginning with the present context for the readers concerning suffering then moving to the past in the example of Christ and finally to a view to the future of the end of all things. In addition, there is an area of intertexture in social texture related to the sacred texture of the formation of religious community. Then, finally, there is an area of ideological texture in the discussion of power.

The repetitive texture develops with related sets of words sometimes in conjunction with each other and sometimes in opposition. The first two set repetitive words are "God" and "Christ" which are used extensively throughout this section. Here we find a pronounced theocentrism with God characterized as the one who saves and provides, whose will is the standard for life, who vindicates the faithful, and to whom glory is due (Green, 2007). The focus of the believer, even in suffering, is the presence and the glory of God. The Christian life is to be lived in Christ rather than like the Gentiles, and this life is based in Christ's redemptive sufferings and the example of Christ in suffering to vindication and glory (Green, 2007). Life is then theocentric and Christocentric with a different focus and center than life in the old way. This life purpose is not to avoid suffering but is to follow Christ and bring glory to God.

The next sets of words that work together are "good" or "right" and "suffer." Peter said it is better to suffer for doing good rather than for doing what is wrong. Doing good now is better than suffering later for doing evil, at the judgment day. This fits the eschatological content of this section and suffering may be God's will if it will produce a good result and the verb here could be translated "if he will it to be so" indicating that if it was God's will for Christ to suffer this could also be for His followers (Witherington, 2007). The point is not that God wills suffering, but that God wills doing what is right rather than doing what is wrong even when it results in suffering (Elliot, 2000). Peter's affirmation is meant to be an encouragement because if suffering is within God's will it is also within His sovereign control, so it is under the will of the Lord not men, and suffering is inevitable whenever Christian faith encounters opposition (Jobes, 2005). Suffering comes from the opposition of men, but it is under God's control. Suffering is not an imperative but it is inevitable as long as the believer is in this world. At first sight this seems contradictory, but it is not. Instead, it provides a nuance of truth concerning suffering. Suffering will come but its inevitability has to do with living in this world and it seems that evil men are in charge but they are not, for God uses suffering for good like in the example of Christ. This is innocent suffering for doing what is right as modeled by Christ in obedience to the Father's will that has God's approval and the person will be vindicated by God as Christ was vindicated (Elliot, 2000). The suffering of God's people is not God's usual will for them but His unusual will and if He permits suffering it for the good of the believer (Hiebert, 1992). It is suffering for doing good but it also involves the will of God, the example of Christ, and the final judgment, so this is not an issue of human injustice, it is an issue with ramifications both for life present and future. Just as suffering was part of the redemptive process in Christ, so suffering is part of the process of life and growth in the believer.

The final sets of repetitive words are "flesh" and "spirit" which are used in opposition to each other. The antithesis is between flesh and spirit and in Verse 18 the flesh refers to Christ in His human sphere of life and spirit refers to His resurrected sphere of life (Blum, 1981). The flesh is the mode of existence of unregenerate humanity in the New Testament and spirit is the mode of living for the regenerate or those pleasing to God (Davids, 1990). In Verse 18, the word "flesh," when referring to Christ, refers to the physical mortal dimension of life and "spirit" refers to the spiritual state of Christ's existence (Elliot, 2000). There is a dichotomy between flesh and spirit in the context of this pericope, though not between phenomenal and noumenal or physical and nonphysical nor between a person's soul and body. Instead, the separation is between a form of existence related to humanity and a form of existence related to the spirit as understood through the resurrection of Jesus Christ. Christ, the example, was put to death in the flesh but made alive in the spirit. The believer then arms themselves to suffer in the flesh to live in the will of God and ultimately live in the spirit. Those who are now dead but had the gospel preached to them may now live in the realm of the spirit regardless of how they were judged by human standards (Jobes, 2005). The believer is to live in the flesh—this human life—armed with the purpose of suffering and living for the will of God ultimately living in the spirit. Life is to be lived looking forward with understanding or wisdom from the past.

In this inner texture, there are also two segments of opening–middle–closing texture in this pericope. The first is found in a chiastic structure in the context of the explanation of the suffering of Christ. The opening has two sections concerning the suffering of Christ. The first phrase is "Christ has suffered in the flesh" and the second in the opening is "arm yourselves with the same purpose." The first phrase is what was divinely done and the second is the essential human response concerning the suffering of Christ. The middle section is the explanation or the reason for this imitation "because He who has suffered has ceased from sin." Then the closing has two sections similar to the opening. The first phrase picks up the concept of the human response with "live the rest of the time in the flesh no longer in the lusts of men" and the final phrase brings in the divine component like the first phrase "for the will of God." This structure can be seen in Figure 4.

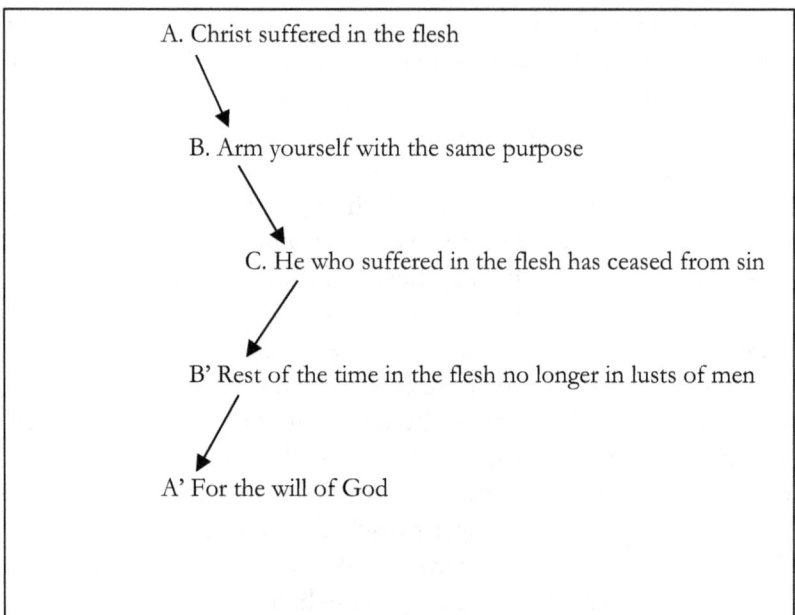

Figure 4. The chiastic structure of 1 Peter 4:1-2

The focus of this rhetorical structure is the middle or the explanation of the whole event of why one should be armed in this way. One that is armed with the purpose or the understanding of suffering in the flesh or in this present life in that he that has suffered in the flesh has ceased from sin and is able to live for the will of God. This is a plea for the believers to arm themselves with the resolve and wisdom that Christ had when He suffered and, since suffering is preferred to sinning, one should be armed with the same attitude because it is better to suffer than sin and face final judgment (Witherington, 2007). Suffering for Christ may happen as a believer and if it does it is better to suffer now in the flesh than to suffer judgment. Suffering causes the believer to cease from sinning (Witherington, 2007). To cease from sin comes from suffering in the flesh, this is then an issue that changes a person in the inner man. Peter's reference to "the one who suffers is through with sin" is the believer armed with the same resolve as Christ which is similar to Philippians 2 in having the same attitude of Christ and it means that those who suffer unjustly because of their faith have demonstrated that they are through with sin by choosing obedience even if it means suffering (Jobes, 2005). This unjust suffering is an outward indicator of a resolve or attitude in the believer to imitate Jesus in following Him. This concept is related to a broad concept in that suffering has a disciplining function and assists in the control of the flesh which is prone to sinning. The author was not claiming that a suffering person atones for their own sin or that it even purifies from sin but rather that suffering, particularly when it is innocent suffering, disciplines the body by which sinning is carried out and thereby trains one to cease from sinning (Elliot, 2000). This training readies one to move away from sin as an outworking of the internal change wrought by suffering. Suffering changes an individual and one armed with the mindset of obedience even in suffering engages life not only with a changed attitude but also a changed perspective and way of living. This makes sense in 1 Peter as a whole where the need to persevere and thus to suffer is the focus (Davids, 1990). The example of Christ shows that one must go through suffering while living in the flesh before one will be finished with sin at death and the believer armed with this insight will live accordingly (Davids, 1990). This suffering and even this insight about suffering changes the life of the believer ontologically in perception of reality and in the inner man. Here "the flesh" is not used in the Pauline sense of the sinful nature but in the normal Jewish sense of human existence as weak and fallen subject to pain and death so individuals in their human existence can live their life here for human desires or for the will of God (Davids, 1990). This change is based on the imitation of Christ in suffering, though it is not redemptive in the believer, it is ontological, and it brings change in perception, attitude, and the way of life; it is a desire change.

There is a second inner texture of the opening–middle–closing structure in this pericope. It is found in the exhortation concerning the nearness of the end. The beginning is the declaration that the end is near. The middle section is the section that explains what one should do based on this reality which begins with the word "therefore." The closing explains the purpose of these exhortations with the words "so that" and then speaking of God's glory. In the middle section of explanation, there are two sets of explanation. The first section explains generally what all believers should do in light of this eschatological reality whereas the second section gives instructions to individual believers and how they should use their specific gifting from God.

The coming of Jesus had inaugurated the last days and from that point onward everything should be seen in light of the end and this manifestation of the kingdom of God in Jesus Christ was the first stage of in the complex event of the end of the old order (Marshall, 1991). The resurrection signaled the end of the old and the beginning of a new age; the age of the end had begun. It is quite likely that this end that Peter referred to had already begun in that when Jesus was raised from the dead, the end times began or it could mean that the completion of all things had arrived (Witherington, 2007). Either way the completion or the end had arrived and it was in process at this very moment, therefore it affects how one lives. For Peter, the goal of God's saving purpose was at hand and this statement registered the present as "the end" but clarified "the end" as a process that will reach its completion at the final judgment (Green, 2007). This is a tension of two realities that meet in the present of the end yet to come at the final judgment and the end that is upon us in the present. "The end" implies not only cessation of, but also the goal toward which the present age moves and the verb "is near" is used in the New Testament concerning the approach of the kingdom of God in relation to the first as well as the second advent of Christ (Hiebert, 1992). The rule or kingdom of God is both present and future and the end is the process between these two events. The end is near in the same way that the kingdom of God is near. This eschatological exhortation functions as a basic image for making sense of Christian experience and a lens through which to see daily life, being comprised of beliefs and values for the Christian believer and community which will give rise to certain behaviors (Green, 2007). This eschatological mindset is an internal issue involving values and beliefs that impact the behavior of the believers. This sense of the impending *eschaton* or the imminent in-breaking of the full and final rule of God conditions all New Testament teaching and without this understanding the radical ethical stance of the literature would hardly be understandable (Davis, 1990). This "present and coming end" impacts the values of individuals resulting in certain behaviors that contain spiritual as well as ethical issues.

The first middle section exhorts the believers in the areas of prayer, love, and hospitality. However, each of the three issues receives some explanation or qualification. In light of the nearness of the end, the believers are to prepare themselves mentally with mental toughness and alertness and a connection with God through prayer (Green, 2007). "Clear-minded was used for a person in his right mind, one who was reasonable and prudent, and the second verb denotes sobriety, to remain alert in order to pray more effectively (Hiebert, 1992). The goal is to continue in prayer and to continue a connection with God that is coupled with being alert and reasonable. In other words, it is incumbent upon the believer to be connected with God and use wisdom and clarity in walking out this connection to God.

The second issue is that of love. The kind of love that is called for here is love that endures and is flexible, and this covering a multitude of sins is not a veiling of sins or atonement for sins but a love that overwhelms and overrides a multitude of sins because Christian love forgives and overlooks a multitude of sins (Witherington, 2007). This love entails a group ethos of loyalty and is a disposition of favoring others in the community with a commitment to harmony in the group (Green, 2007). This kind of love extinguishes sin and its effects within the community by not retaliating in kind, realizing within the community this way of dealing with sin and enabling the community to survive (Jobes, 2005). Love brings the dynamic of commitment in the context of community in daily living.

The third issue is that of hospitality. *Hospitality* describes one who has an affectionate concern for strangers, even offering them food and shelter and this was highly valued in the early church as an expression of love and was considered a necessary qualification for a leader in the church (Hiebert, 1992). In this context, hospitality is a practical expression of love as taught in the preceding verse and a means of maintaining cohesion in the community. This was a highly regarded virtue in the ancient world, especially in opening ones home to others and the sign of generous and honorable families (Elliot, 2000). Hospitality is a practical expression of love and further builds cohesion in the community as an expression of generosity and honor.

In the middle section of this inner texture the emphasis shifts to exhortations to individuals in the community. The final resource for preservation of the Christian community is the stewardship of the gifts of God's grace for serving others with the implication that each believer has received a gift for his or her service to others (Jobes, 2005). Each believer has a gift that comes from God's grace and it is to be used to serve. Peter indicated that there are many such gifts but he only focused on two major sorts of gifts: speaking and doing or serving (Witherington, 2007). Those who speak in teaching about Christ or offer counsel in His name must understand themselves to be representing God's words to the community. They are engaged in serious business so they must speak in accordance with God's revelation not from narrow individuality (Jobes, 2005). If speaking as the words of God, their speech must bear the character of God's word (Witherington, 2007). Speaking is a gift of grace from God when one speaks as from God and it is not just narrow but it is representing God's speech to the community. This rendering service is a very broad category including any kind of helping or encouraging for the benefit of the church and comes from the strength God supplies not from human energy or for one's own status (Grudem, 1999). The gifts of grace are used for the community and not the status of the individual and these gifts bring benefit to the community and glory to God.

The closing section of this texture explains the purpose of these responses to the eschatological reality upon the community of believers. The purpose of Christian service is that through it Jesus Christ God will be glorified because people will praise Him for His grace that comes to them through His followers (Blum, 1981). Now God is to be glorified because of the acts of the believers, but it is expressly through Jesus Christ, showing that it is not human institutions but Jesus is the one who holds ultimate power and the one to who honor is due (Green, 2007). Each individual believer has a gift and must be faithful in using that gift to benefit others in the community and to bring honor to Jesus Christ, not to self, and this gift is not the result of human effort but of the grace of God.

In this context of inner texture, there is also a social intertexture of a term or concept used in forming religious community which is an item of sacred texture. In these verses in Chapter 4 of 1 Peter, the author was forming religious community and in this context he used a picture that can be seen in the social texture of the era of this writing. The picture is that of a steward. A steward is one who takes care of a house and the function of steward in the church probably grew out of the "house steward" who administered the household in these early house churches (Witherington, 2007). This was a domestic steward, a reliable slave who managed a household as seen in Pagan, Jewish, and Christian writings and this person had authority delegated by the householder (Elliot, 2000). This was a common term or concept for the people of this time period. In many contexts the church is envisioned as household and the leaders as responsible household stewards. In the network of house churches that comprised early Christianity, this kind of household agent would have been familiar (Elliot, 2000). The inference is that all believers should use the gifts of grace to be stewards of the gifts, and the two gifts mentioned are the gifts that are used in leading the household of God: speaking and serving. Yet this picture would be familiar in the settings of the house churches of the era. Steward was an individual entrusted with administrative responsibility of the household affairs (Hiebert, 1992). By analogy, this includes all believers, but by application, would be instruction to leaders as well especially in the context of the household picture of the church and the literal setting of the church in houses in this era in history.

There is also a progressive texture found in the larger pericope concerning the element of time. In 3:13-22, the present suffering and salvation are discussed. Then in 4:1-6, the past is discussed in the past suffering of Christ and the past life of the believer and the past preaching of the gospel. Finally, in 4:7-11 is the instruction in how to live in the present in light of the future or the eschatological reality of the present. This progression ends with stating the purpose of this progression in the life of the believer—that God would be glorified through Jesus Christ who has the true power to rule. This serves as a conclusion of the textual unit as well as of this section wherein praise to God through Jesus Christ is for His mighty acts of salvation and is a disclosure of God's character and purpose and the one who has honor and power (Green, 2007).

This power to rule brings an ideological texture into the discussion. Though God has all rule and power and honor, He brings salvation through suffering and delivers His people through suffering. God uses power paradoxically, not as a king though He has a kingdom, but as a suffering servant shepherd who leads through suffering and gives a picture of leading as a household servant. Perhaps the all-powerful God uses power differently that those with limited power. If this is so, then it is imperative that mortals learn the proper, divine use of power within its proper limits. God's power is infinite and He is not limited to what He has actually done; He is able to do more than He does and though we do not have infinite power God has given us power to bring about results and in various kinds of authority structures and the proper use of power in ways consistent with His will brings glory to God as it reflects His character (Grudem, 1994). Therefore, it is imperative to learn this proper use of power. The inner texture of 1 Peter 3:13 – 4:11 can be seen in Table 11.

Table 11: Inner Texture of 1 Peter 3:13-4:11

Vs.	Repetitive	Opening–middle–closing	Progressive
3:13	Good		Present
3:14	Suffer		3:13-3:22
3:15	Christ		
3:16	Good (2x), Christ		
3:17	God, suffer, good (right)		
3:18	Christ, God, flesh, spirit		
3:19	Spirits		Now
3:20	God		
3:21	Flesh, Christ, good		Now
3:22	God		
4:1	Christ, suffer, flesh (2x)	O—Christ suffered	4:1-4:6
4:1		O—arm with same mind	
4:1		M—He who has suffered	
4:2	God, flesh	C—live rest of the time	
4:2		C—will of God	
4:3			Past
4:6	God, spirit, flesh		
4:7	Spirit	O—end is near	Future
4:7		M—therefore general	4:7-4:11
4:10	God	M—each one	Eschaton
4:11	God (3x), Christ	C—in order that	

In this pericope, leadership is seen in the picture of steward as one who administrates the household and who is faithful in the use of the gifts of grace. Leaders need to be effective in the use of their gifts that they have been given to them in speaking and serving. In addition, these gifts are given divinely and are not to develop the status or honor of the individual; instead they are to bring glory to God. This steward leader is under the authority of the Lord but is responsible to faithfully use the gifts to serve and benefit the community. The leader is to serve the community. As a member of the community, a leader must be reasonable and clear minded, and must love in practical ways that are manifest in serving the community such as hospitality. Those who successfully follow the Lord must learn to live for the will of God and arm themselves with the mentality of suffering as a part of the growth and change process. Suffering and even insight about suffering changes one ontologically in perception of reality and in the inner man. This change is based on the imitation of Christ in suffering, though it is not redemptive, it is ontological and it brings change in perception, attitude, and the way of life; it is a desire change. This is an important change for a leader to be effective in the community to lead from reality rather than simply from behavior.

In light of the *eschaton,* the leader must have values that are affected by the coming end impacting the ethics of the person and the leadership of the person. Then it must be noticed that God though all powerful uses His power paradoxically. To bring redemption He sent Jesus to suffer and die and to help His people He brings them through suffering. The leader must learn to use power properly like God uses power to bring glory to God and reveal His character. These are all issues of internal change, reality, and virtue which are issues of the person and the inner person, not simply of behavior. Therefore, they are ontological in nature but manifest in behavior that has impact on others.

Do not be surprised at the fiery ordeal among you, which comes upon you for your testing, as though some strange thing were happening to you.
  Peter, NASB

CHAPTER 12

I PETER – PERICOPE 4

1 Peter 4:12-19

In this section, the issue of suffering is addressed again and pressed further in its reconfiguration from past standards or concepts for suffering. This pericope indicates that the believers were surprised by their fiery trials and it means they were habitually surprised and Peter was once again drawing on the image of metals being refined by fire and we do have a particular theme here or *exposito* on suffering and looking at it from different angles (Witherington, 2007). If suffering is understood in why it happens then there can be rejoicing. There are two sides to it: first, suffering for Christ finds its significance in Christ's suffering for us and one day we will share in glory with Him, while secondly, suffering purifies the believer and these trials are the beginning of God's work of renewal (Clowney, 1988). Suffering was reconfigured in Chapter 1 of 1 Peter but it is now examined again with greater force and understanding for the believers who had been surprised by this suffering. Peter made the startling claim that suffering should come as no surprise to the believer; it is actually an opportunity for joy and he opened in this section with the thought that it was to be expected and ends with an admonition to continue to trust God and live righteously in suffering (Jobes, 2005). Suffering continues to be reconfigured as a source of growth, but even further as a source of joy.

This short section contains a repetitive inner texture, aesthetic–sensory inner texture, along with an opening–middle–closing texture. In addition, there is a recontextualization from Hebrew Scripture in intertexture and the reconfiguration already mentioned concerning suffering. The repetitive structure contains the words "you," "God," "suffer," "glory," and "rejoice." The opening–middle–closing texture opens with a call to the beloved, then an exhortation to them concerning suffering containing the key words "if," "make," "sure," and "for," and final closing with a "therefore" statement. The aesthetic–sensory texture is found in the words that evoke different, even surprising, senses in the context of suffering. This aesthetic texture resides predominantly in the range of the senses that the text evokes or embodies and it may give color and tone to the other textures in the text (Robbins, 1996). This is found in the joyful response to suffering and in other words that embody different senses like surprise, not ashamed, reviled, and exultation.

In this section, there are two sets of repetitive words that are connected to each other. The first set concerns the believer with words like "you" in that it is directed to this community; it is personal and relevant to their context. The author had a particular stress on "you" showing that this is not simply a general teaching about suffering but is concerned with the suffering of the addressees in particular (Elliot, 2000). In Verse 12, the threefold use of the word "you" is a clear example of reduplication for the sake of emphasis and the hearers are being urged to respond to their suffering (Witherington, 2007). Whereas in the prophecy of Isaiah the spirit of God rests on the Messiah, Peter wrote that the Spirit of God rests on "you" (plural), interpreting suffering through an exegesis that confirms the status of the hearers as the messianic community in the grand purpose of God (Green, 2007). This is not just a generic concept of suffering, it is particular and personal and those who suffer are encouraged to respond well as a community and walk in the purpose of God. Suffering is personal, but as has been seen, it is filled with opportunities for change and development as individuals and as a community.

The other two words in this set are "suffering" and "rejoice." Though not normally joined together, these become important connections in this pericope. Suffering is not to be considered as something foreign to the Christian experience, but rather, as a refining test as found in the words "fiery ordeal" as a metaphor out of the Greek Old Testament for the refining of metals. In distinction to the normal response to suffering of shock, the believer is to rejoice because of participating in the sufferings of Christ (Blum, 1981). This concept of the fiery ordeal sets the stage for the explanation and exhortation concerning suffering and its connection to rejoicing. Here is an *exposito* or a rhetorical development of a certain theme in that of suffering with the announcement of the theme as that of "fiery trials" (Witherington, 2007). The author opened with the thought that such suffering is expected and closed with an admonition concerning suffering and living righteously as an expression of trust in God with the theme of rejoicing amid trials in anticipation of final joy (Jobes, 2005). This repetition and connection of these two words forms the theme for this section.

One is not to be surprised by suffering in a fiery trial since it is for testing and not something that is an anomaly. The author invited the audience to see their suffering from several angles in its nature as honorable, in the etiology of suffering, in the presence of God in suffering, in the meaning of suffering in the divine plan, and proper responses to suffering (Green, 2007). These multiple aspects of suffering from divine perspective gave a view of reality that is contrary to the norm and socially accepted realities concerning suffering. Peter was drawing on the image of refining metals as a testing that reveals the genuineness of faith in the person (Witherington, 2007). This suffering does not destroy the person, it purifies since it is the purging fire of discipline (Clowney, 1988). Suffering is a process of testing and refining the person. This image of the refiner's fire suggests that this suffering purifies and strengthens the believer, to prove the person, which is a word used in a positive sense of a trial that is expected to have a positive outcome (Grudem, 1999). This testing is not for failure but for success with a view to increased faith, purity, and faithfulness. It is not destructive; it is positive and constructive in building one's life, particularly the inner life.

The believers also share the sufferings of Christ. This suffering is an indication of believers' identification with Christ and a reimaging of suffering as identification with Him in a type of imitation in how they respond to suffering and in obtaining an eschatological perspective on their suffering (Davids, 1990). In suffering in the context of Christ's suffering, there is a new identity and a new perspective found. As one suffers for Christ that person is linked to Him and partakes of the sufferings of Christ not in contributing to redemption but by following in His steps; this reinforces the reality of belonging to Christ (Clowney, 1988). This suffering brings a new reality to come to the fore in one's life as well as a new perspective that brings rejoicing. The reason for this rejoicing now in the midst of suffering is that when Christ appears in glory the believer will be able to rejoice as one honored by Christ as one who persevered (Witherinton, 2007). This joy is not only a future hope but a present reality and suffering is seen positively as a divine testing and as a reason for rejoicing and this present rejoicing is a prelude to joy at the final revelation of Christ's glory (Elliot, 2000). The believer imitates Christ in the context of suffering and rejoices in the present as well looks forward to future joy. Joy and suffering come together in the present whereas joy is anticipated in the future.

It is here that the concept of suffering is connected to the other two repetitive words of "God" (Christ) and "glory." The redundancy of the phrase "the Spirit of glory and of God" is typical of this type of rhetoric and is done to amplify the effect of the majesty of that which is being described (Witherington, 2007). The future speaks of the coming revelation of glory wherein the believer will rejoice but in the present the spirit of God and glory rests on the believer who is reviled or suffers rejection. If one is reviled here is a standard term for verbal abuse and public shaming and is a term of scorn or insult indicating that this suffering may have been in the form of verbal abuse and public humiliation (Elliot, 2000). This verbal abuse or humiliation for Christ for the name of Christ brings blessing and glory. The glory in Verse 13 was future, but here it is present, indicating an unusual and powerful presence of the Holy Spirit to bless and strengthen the individual (Grudem, 1999). Being verbally abused in suffering for Christ is a specific way of suffering that brings not only present joy but present glory as well. The added glory is consistent with the stress on glory in this section and may have been prompted by the desire to ground the addressees honor in the honor (glory) of God linking glory and suffering (Elliot, 2000). Suffering, instead of bringing shame, seen from the proper reality brings honor instead of shame and strength rather than destruction as well as joy instead of surprise.

Do not suffer for evil is the only negative instruction concerning suffering. The author here hastened to add that not all who suffer should consider themselves blessed; no Christian should consider suffering as a common criminal and adding a further category of evil activity of that of a meddler as one who meddles in things that do not concern him (Davids, 1990). Whereas the preceding nouns refer to stock types of unacceptable behavior, this one is unique and appears nowhere else in all of Greek literature while some would interpret it having to do with a bishop particularly having to do with misleading the flock and it may be related to the word for another kind of overseer—an improper overseer (Elliot, 2000). Though the concept is not clear due to lack of comparative words, it is still a significant word in this context. At the very least this form of the word involves a combination of the word for overseer and some form of the word meaning belonging to another or strange (Elliot, 2000). It literally has the sense of overseeing the affairs of others but with this activity not being the proper concern of the doer (Witherington, 2007). Do not suffer for apparent evil or for becoming an improper overseer. The focus has been the household of God and the previous section was about an excellent steward whereas now there is a warning not to become an improper overseer and even to relate suffering for this kind of activity as some kind of honor.

In Verse 16, the concept of suffering is again connected to glory to God but only as one suffers as a believer. Suffering as a Christian contrasts with suffering as an evildoer; those who suffer as followers of Christ should not be ashamed, but it is an opportunity for honoring and glorifying God (Elliot, 2007). In 4:16, Peter contrasted shame with glory when one is suffering for Christ and provided an alternate way of honor in the midst of an honor and shame society (Jobes, 2005). This innocent suffering as a Christian is the true way to honor in contradistinction to the societal norms of the time. These are positive valuations of innocent suffering: it is a divine test, it is a sign of unity with the suffering of Christ, it is a cause for rejoicing, a mark of the Spirit's presence, and an opportunity for actively glorifying God (Elliot, 2007). Suffering is paramount in this textual unit, with Peter drawing together and then extending the threads of this letter developing a proper response (Green, 2007). The proper response involves walking through the suffering with joy and honor as they grow as persons as believers and even as stewards in God's household.

In this pericope Christ, Spirit, and God are used rapidly as well as repetitively discussing the sufferings of Christ, the Spirit of glory, glory to God as well as the household of God, the gospel of God, and the will of God. At the end of this section, the final three aspects of that which is God's come together. The household of God who obey the gospel of God and those who suffer according to the will of God should entrust their souls to God. This theocentricity shifts the focus of suffering from shame to honor with God in the context of the household of God which is judged by God first. Peter assumed that his readers would be judged with the rest of humanity and this thought was informed by the tradition of Judaism in that when God judges He will begin with His own people and in fact with the elders in the temple, and this concept comes from images of the Old Testament as God's presence as a refining fire (Jobes, 2005). The sense of this word for judgment is that God will begin His process of judging humanity with His own people who have come to Christ and this is not a word of condemnation but of the action of the judge with no penalty in view (Jobes, 2005). This judgment also purifies the believers encouraging them not to walk in shameful behavior (Marshall, 1991). The judging begins with the testing of the believers who will be purified and glorify God, but then it will move on to unbelievers who have no foundation in the judgment. Compared to the judgment of unbelievers, the judgment of believers will be mild (Marshall, 1991). The testing of persecution is eschatological in that it sorts out those who are truly Christ's from those who are not and yet in the end those who do not know Christ will suffer even more in judgment (Jobes, 2005). This testing begins with believers in the present but continues in judgment for the rest of humanity.

Lastly, the suffering is modified by the will of God, or according to the will of God. Peter regarded such suffering for Christ as suffering according to the will of God, not in suffering for its own sake but because there is no other way for evil to be overcome (Witherington, 2007). This is seen as well in the sufferings of Christ this were His way of overcoming not just evil in context but of overcoming evil innately. Suffering is not to deflect the believer because it is part of the calling in Christ, and the nexus of suffering and honor is embodied in Jesus Christ Himself (Jobes, 2005). In suffering one overcomes evil and it is part of the calling in the imitation of Christ and in accordance with the will of God. As this occurs to believers, they are to entrust their souls to their Creator. The word here for entrust literally refers to placing one's life in the hands of another (Witherington, 2007) or to make a deposit (Elliot, 2000). The inner attitude in doing this is one of trust in handing one's self to God (Davids, 1990). In suffering one enters new levels of trust in God.

In this inner texture, the combination of words shows the connection between suffering, joy, glory, God, and the individual. Suffering is part of the will of God which brings about trust, an imitation of Christ, testing, purifying and glory to God with blessing, and glory resting on the individual, and is a cause of rejoicing. Christians in no way should be surprised at their suffering since they are in communion with Christ who suffered and their suffering affects solidarity with Christ bearing witness to Him. It is a cause of rejoicing and joy with a rich presence of the Spirit (Witherington, 2007). Suffering is a paradoxical work seeming to bring opposition and destruction wherein reality brings joy, affirmation, and growth. This judgment or testing begins in the household of God probably with the leaders. The leaders are warned not to lead as those who mislead and this judgment in the household will bring change and growth in one's trust, faith, and imitation of Christ.

In this short section concerning suffering, there is also an aesthetic texture in the surprising responses that are to come from suffering. These responses include not to be surprised at the paradox of suffering, finding that it is in the will of God, not just that it happens. When one is found in identifying with Christ in suffering the person is to rejoice; again in this paradox of suffering though painful produces new identity. Further, though the normal course of suffering would cause shame one is not to be ashamed and conversely glorify or honor God. Then once one has the epiphany that all of this suffering is in accordance with the will of God one is to move to new levels of complete trust in God. It was God's will that Christ should suffer to redeem His people and the need arose because of evil in the world, but in a world where evil exists its defeat is only possible through suffering, evil cannot be wiped out but must be overcome through the suffering love of God, this is part of the mystery of evil (Marshall, 1991). In the theology of the cross, God revealed His power through weakness and suffering by overcoming evil by death and suffering (Althaus, 1966). This paradox of suffering deeply affects the person and suffering brings change that overcomes evil especially as one learns to embrace it paradoxically in rejoicing, trusting, and glorifying God.

In addition, there is an opening–middle–closing texture here that reinforces these concepts of suffering. The opening begins with an exhortation concerning attitude toward testing. This section begins with "beloved" indicating a beginning of a new section and a final conclusion drawn from the Old Testament (Witherington, 2007). The author opened a new section with a direct and yet intimate address to his readers and this unit of 4:12-19 begins with an injunction and substantiation then ends in Verse 19 with a final injunction (Elliot, 2000). The middle section gives instruction about suffering using words like "if" and "make sure" in directing the believers concerning suffering. This is a series of imperatival statements concerning positive and negative types of suffering and motivation in suffering (Elliot, 2000). Ultimately believers should not be surprised by suffering and opposition but through the process finally come to new levels of trust and purpose of living in the will of God. These counterintuitive processes are not suggestions but imperatives for those in the household of God.

Finally, intertexture suffering is not only recontextualized in this new eschatological reality, but also Old Testament concepts of judgment are brought forward and interpreted in light of the church's reality of suffering. Peter interpreted present hostility and suffering through an exegesis that confirmed the status of the audience as the messianic community. Suffering for the sake of Christ finds its meaning in Isaiah's messianic ruler in 11:2, 12, but in Isaiah the Spirit of God rests on Him, while in Peter, the Spirit of God rests on all believers (Green, 2007). The Spirit of the Lord on the Messiah in the Old Testament is now the Spirit of the Lord that rests on the community. The community becomes identified with this messianic leader upon whom the Spirit rests. In addition, in Verse 18, Proverbs 11:31 recontextualizes the eschatological judgment of God more specifically into Peter's theology of messianic woes (Green, 2007). Peter tried to give the audience some perspective so they would see what was happening to them in an eschatological perspective and as part of the larger history (Witherington, 2007). The Old Testament text concerning judgment against the ungodly was brought into the readers present as a view to the future of judgment in light of the present reality of suffering. Peter wanted them to see the present in light of the future for a proper perspective of the present as well as the past in the sufferings of Christ. An ability to perceive the future assisted the proper understanding of reality for the present for the household of God and the individual believer. The inner texture of this pericope can be seen graphically in Table 12.

Table 12: Inner Texture of 1 Peter 4:12-19

Vs.	Repetitive	Opening–middle–closing	Aesthetic
4:12	Trial, you (2x)	Opening—beloved	Not surprised
4:13	Suffering, rejoice (2x)		Rejoice
4:13	Christ, you(2x), glory		Exultation
4:14	Christ, Spirit, God, glory		
4:14	You (2x)	Middle—if you	Blessed
4:15	Suffer, you	Middle—make sure	
4:16	Suffer, glory, God	Middle—if anyone	Not ashamed
4:17	God (2x)	Middle—for, if	
4:18		Middle—if it is	
4:19	Suffer, God	Ending—therefore	Entrust

Concerning leadership, there are several salient issues in this short pericope. Suffering is paradoxical; though it appears to bring negative things into a group and individuals, just the opposite is true when properly embraced and understood. This is not just a random exhortation; it is an exhortation to the household of God where judgment begins with the leaders. This judgment is not in the form of penalty but in testing. This testing when embraced in a new identity with Christ brings change that is internal and powerful. It brings purification, strength, and joy. Understanding and embracing suffering can be a source for character development as well as leadership development in ontological issues of the leader. In responding properly to suffering, trust is also a result which could be a further needed ingredient for leadership. These leaders are told not to mislead the followers, to be persons of integrity. In the context of suffering there is the imitation of Christ which is a key component in understanding and living in the paradox of suffering. Peter was concerned that the community would see the future properly to give a true perspective of the present; therein a proper vision of the future and how it impinged the present was important for the household of God and therefore a key ingredient for the leaders.

Therefore humble yourselves under the mighty hand of God, that He may exalt you at the proper time.
   Peter, NASB

CHAPTER 13

1 PETER – PERICOPE 5

1 Peter 5:1-7
This chapter of 1 Peter is separated differently by different authors, with Witherington (2007) and Green (2007) putting the first five verses together and Marshall (1991) putting the first four verses together and then Grudem (1999) putting the first seven verses together in a section. For the sake of consistency with sociorhetorical interpretation, the first seven verses were considered together leaving Verses 8-14 of Chapter 5 to be considered as the final section of this text.

In this section, Peter assumed that there will be leaders in the church and it is the style of leadership that is the issue in the way in which leadership is exercised and the question is whether this reflects a culturally determined style or whether they are timeless instructions (Marshall, 1991). This question is the crux of the matter for leadership studies in 1 Peter. If they are culturally driven, then we can adjust with the culture, but if they are not, there may be a warning here to examine these issues carefully for insight that comes from the context of timeless reality rather than constantly changing cultural context. According to Marshall (1991), these instructions are timeless in their relevance. However, the question still remains as to how these timeless truths can be applied into a new context since the truths are wrapped in cultural language understood by the recipients of this document, 1 Peter.

It is significant that this exhortation to leadership follows the section on suffering and the household of God. The previous exhortation included a warning against suffering as an improper leader. The concept is that of an irresponsible bishop or leader (Jobes, 2005). Then this section follows with an exhortation to responsible leadership. This exhortation to the elders follows the explanation of the sorting process in the church where judgment begins with the elders who are in front of the temple and here Peter applied this as he moved from judgment in the household to elders and these two thoughts are joined here (Jobes, 2005). Leadership is an important issue in this text as ties some of the arguments together and it is the crowning argument in dealing with the situation of the readers. This pericope begins with a conjunctive connecting it to the last section with an explanation of how one would express a privileged position of leadership since honor before God is not an excuse for the exercise of privileged status over others (Green, 2007). This is not an afterthought at the end of the text or an addendum. This section is about leadership functions and the earlier section on priesthood of believers in no way rules out individuals being singled out as leaders (Witherington, 2007). This function of leadership includes not only activities but attitudes as well issues of the inner person and like the last section are paradoxical in nature. Though one is a leader, this person must be careful to not use privileged status in this leadership.

In this pericope are found several structures of inner texture; repetitive, progressive, narrational, and opening–middle–closing. The repetitions in this section include" elder(s)," "glory," "shepherd," "flock," "humility," and "God." The progressive texture begins with instructions to elders with a reference to glory then moving to using the picture of shepherd for the leader but still connected to glory and then finally to all, not just leaders, and the idea of exaltation. The narrational texture moves from personal imperative in "therefore I exhort" in verse 1 to instruction to leaders in Verses 2-3 to discussion of reward in Verse 4 then back to instruction to all instead of just the leaders in Verse 5 and then a return to a personal imperative in Verse 6 in "therefore humble yourselves." The opening–middle–closing texture is found in a chiastic structure that spans the entire section with a focus on Verse 4 and the reward of a crown of glory.

In addition, there is an issue of intertexture of culture as seen earlier in the text but it receives new focus and amplification here in the picture of a shepherd as a leader. Finally, there is an ideological texture concerning the issue of power found in three tightly connected contrasts in this pericope. Each of these textures is connected to leadership just as in the previous section the textures were connected to suffering.

Two of the words in the repetitive texture here directly address leaders. These two words are "elder" and "shepherd." Both of these words are filled with cultural significance for the recipients of this document. Both of these concepts are echoes from the Old Testament that are recontextualized for leaders in the context of the church. In addition, the word "God" is also related to these words in this section. Peter's instruction began with an exhortation to shepherd the flock of God that is among them. This concept of shepherding comes from Old Testament leadership constructs. The concept of the shepherd as applied to leaders among God's people is traditional and it is applied to God and God's leadership style as well as to human leaders in the Old Testament (Witherington, 2007). The picture is of a natural shepherd caring for his sheep, however the leaders in Israel who had been elders, kings, prophets, or even priests were called shepherds and were exhorted by the Lord to shepherd the people of God in Jeremiah 23:1-40. This imagery of shepherding and sheep runs deeply into Israel's Scripture and is significant in that it relativizes the role of the elders in that they are called to exercise authority but within the limits of God's purpose exemplified in Christ (Green, 2007). The Lord is the shepherd of His people according to Psalm 23:1 and He called individuals to become human shepherds to lead His people (Ezekiel 34:30-31, Jeremiah 23:4). The elders are to lead by shepherding the people of God in following the example of the Lord Himself. The Scripture contains a rich texture concerning leading as a shepherd and elders as leaders in the community and this instruction from Peter endeavored to bring together these cultural pictures in explaining leadership for the household of God. This leadership is a leadership that is defined not only by Old Testament settings but also by Christ and how He led since He is the Chief Shepherd.

Though the word for "elder" here could mean an older person, it also was a term for one who functioned as a community leader and the instruction that accompanies this word makes it clear that these are leaders who are addressed here as elders, shepherds, and overseers, and elders existed throughout the Greco-Roman world not just among the Jews (Elliot, 2000). Therefore, this texture would not only be cultural, it would be social as well in the case of the concept of an elder as a leader. In this era, the responsibility of leadership in the Jewish Synagogue was given to the synagogue ruler or an elder (Witherington, 2007). Elder was a normal word or concept used for leader in the traditions of Judaism, in the traditions of the Greco-Roman world, and the contemporary word of this text. These elders or leaders were told to lead by shepherding the flock; concepts not only repeated in this pericope but also with profound significance of the hearers this exhortation. In addition, the repetitive concept of the flock of God is also rich with meaning being recontextualized from Old Testament concepts. The concept of comparing the people of God to a flock of sheep is prominent in the Scriptures for example in Isaiah 53:6-7 and Luke 15:3-7 in a parable comparing people to lost sheep (Blum, 1981). These three words are repeated in this short section and are brought forward from previous Scriptures and applied to the context of leadership in the community of Christ. All of this to say, the role of elder is deeply rooted in the Old Testament and takes its essential character from the nature of God to act in conformity with God's exercise of leadership (Green, 2007).

In this exhortation to leadership, Peter identified with the other leaders calling himself a fellow elder and then identified all of the leaders with Jesus calling Him the Chief Shepherd. The definite article here combined with the adjective *sym* may be understood as possessive, as your fellow elder, one who understands their pressures and responsibilities, and his purpose could be to encourage and console these leaders (Jobes, 2005). It is obvious that Peter was trying to inculcate a collegial relationship with the other leaders here and this is the same kind of leveling language used by Jesus when he talks about the disciples being his brothers (Witherington, 2007). Peter, though a significant leader or apostle is not using privileged status to lead or direct. Peter refused special privilege locating himself as an elder alongside other elders and he was not exercising conventional authority since he was not distributing directives simply on the basis of his apostolic office (Green, 2007). Peter was a leader leading other leaders as he was led by Christ. This could be translated as Shepherd the sheep of God in Verse 2 and uses the same verb as Jesus when He told Peter to tend His sheep (Grudem, 1999). This vocation of tending the sheep given to

Peter by Jesus was now mediated through Peter to these elders (Green, 2007). The picture of shepherd, elder, and flock draws from Scripture a rich picture of leadership that is in imitation of God's leadership and His desire for human leaders. It is futher emphasized in that Christ is held up as the Chief Shepherd. Jesus is called the Chief Shepherd, a term that originally referred to a supervising shepherd who oversees the other shepherds caring for a flock too large for one shepherd to handle; in essence these shepherds have the same task as did Christ (Witherington, 2007). Christian leadership is thus a sharing in the leadership of Christ (Marshall, 1991). The shepherd, elder, and flock image is an image of intentional leadership that is modeled by God, then by Christ, and is to be imitated by the elders as ones leading a flock.

The next set of words give insight into the internal issue of leadership in humility and the result of good leadership as a shepherd, that being glory. Peter used a word here for humility built on the root of one of his favorite terms meaning "to think"; thus, this concerns a frame of mind that belongs to people that are done with positioning themselves in the world's social hierarchy (Green, 2007). Humility is not an appearance or an external disposition as much as an internal mindset that affects one's behavior. "Clothe yourselves" is a rare word referring to a slave putting on an apron before serving like Christ did in girding Himself when He washed the feet of the disciples and believers are to imitate their Lord in being clothed with humility (Blum, 1981). Humility is a mindset, but it is also an intentional act of putting on a certain attitude. This image of clothing oneself with humility is especially close to the action of Jesus at the last supper in preparing to humbly wash the feet of the disciples and this is a call to all the members of the community—leaders and followers (Elliot, 2000). This call to humility was to permeate the community but it was distinctive in its call not just to members but leaders as well. True humility as opposed to contrived, self-degrading humiliation comes from recognizing one's dependence on God and is expressed by recognition of one's role and position in God's economy and this frees one from attempts to gain power and prestige (Jobes, 2005). Humility is not self-loathing but self-recognition and the design to fulfill one's purpose or role rather than endeavor to gain power. This humility is attained by casting all anxieties on the Lord which frees a person from constant concern for self and enabling him or her to truly care for others (Grudem, 1999). True humility is a mindset but it can be developed in one's life. This humility toward one another is tied to humility before God and Peter amplified this need for humility calling the readers to humble themselves, indicating a duty that needed immediate attention, and to trust in God's care (Hiebert, 1992). Humility must be attended to and developed in one's life and part of that process is learning dependence on the Lord. Peter's message to these leaders is one of humility with an emphasis on their role as servant leaders and shepherds of God's flock and they are to care for their followers modeling Christ in every way (Leahy, 2010). The shepherding role, as well as the characteristic of humility, is to be done in imitation of Christ the example. Humility as a virtue became central to the Christian ethic and part of the essence of what it means to be like Christ and Peter told the leaders that they were to model this virtue following the lead of their head shepherd and the Lord would give grace to them so they could go on serving and humbling themselves (Witherington, 2007). In the imitation of Christ, humility is a key issue for leaders who also model it for others to follow. All leadership and followership is to be done in the context of mutual respect and serving one another and when leadership is seen in this way as a form of service in humility we do indeed have a uniquely biblical view of leadership (Witherington, 2007). A key component in this exhortation to leadership is humility, not self-degradation, but a mindset of humility and active service in imitation of Christ.

Glory in this section is seen as a reward. Peter was a witness of the sufferings of Christ and a partaker of the glory to be revealed. Peter described himself as sharing in the coming glory and he implied that he has a share in it now but the glory is yet to be unveiled and this is an example of the present–future tension found in this text (Witherington, 2007). His connection with God involved the past tense as a witness of the sufferings of Christ, and it included the future concerning the glory to be revealed, but notice that it is also present in that he is a partaker of this glory, not that he will be a partaker. The idea that the glory is about to be revealed is related to the expectation of the revelation of Christ and illustrates the future as well as the present orientation of this text. The encouragement to the leaders then is not just about the present work, it is also about the future and the rewards of the future. This future view was not only for Peter, but also for all of the leaders who would receive an unfading crown of glory. The reward of faithful leadership will be a crown of glory that never fades; the crown is a well-known image in the first-century as a reward for athletic winners and civic benefactors so the victory that is attained through perseverance is an unfading glory (Jobes, 2005). There is a reward for faithful leadership that is glory or honor. The glory that is the honor shared is that of Jesus Christ and it also involves the final glory or honor at the return of Christ (Elliot, 20000). This crown is a special honor given to those worthy of public recognition for special service and this carries the nuance of an outwardly visible evidence of honor, but in the future (Grudem, 1999). The elders are to lead in humility, not using the prerogative of status or position nor to seek that honor; however, honor will be given them in the future as a result of their perseverance and service in leadership.

The progressive texture begins with instructions to elders and a reference to glory then moves to using the picture of shepherd as the leader, but still connected to glory, and then finally to all, including leaders and the idea of exaltation. Possibly the idea of exaltation and glory and reward are connected. Peter began the discussion with his personal participation in the glory to be revealed, then exhorted the leaders to faithful service in the leaders' response to the will of God which has a reward of glory. To this, he added instruction of how to be exalted by God to receive this reward. The point here was not that believers have a choice of whether to humble themselves, the point was how Christians respond under difficult situations accepting them as part of God's work rather than railing against God in order that God may exalt them at the appointed time (Jobes, 2005). Neither the specific time nor the kind of exhortation are specified, so it is best to understand it generally; the time could be in this life or in the life to come and He may exalt an individual in the way that seems best to Him, perhaps in deeper fellowship with Him, perhaps in terms of responsibility, reward, or honor that can be seen by others (Grudem, 1999). This humility to exaltation connects humility and glory or honor as well. Humility brings the reward of exaltation but not from self-seeking and this reward can be eternal future or simply future, it is not the same for everyone but there is reward.

The narrational texture moves from personal imperative in "Therefore I exhort" in Verse 1, to instruction to leaders in Verses 2 and 3, to discussion of reward in Verse 4, then to instruction to all instead of just the leaders in Verse 5, and, finally, to a return to a personal imperative in Verse 6 in "Therefore humble yourselves." This texture reinforces the connection between the exhortation to leaders and the ultimate issue of accepting the work of God in them under God's powerful hand in walking humbly in the midst of the situations in which they find themselves. It is allowing themselves to be humbled with God implied as the one who humbles and this statement is consolatory recalling the great acts of deliverance in the exodus by the hand of God showing His power to protect and deliver His people (Elliot, 2000). God's mighty hand is an image deeply rooted in the Old Testament in connection to the deliverance of Israel, thus the readers are to see God at work behind the scenes and allow themselves to be brought low so that exaltation may come (Davids, 1990). Humility comes from a certain mindset but also comes from receiving the difficult situations as the work of God in humbling and yet preparing the person to be exalted at the right time.

In this texture not only can progression be seen from instructions to reward to the way or process to receive the reward through humility but also this reveals an opening–middle–closing texture in a chiastic structure. This begins with section a personal imperative then the second section is instructions to elders then to discussion of reward in Verse 3. The next section returns to instructions but this time to everyone and then in the final section is the final imperative concerning humility. The center or focus of this chiastic structure is the leaders receiving a crown of glory of reward for leading well. To lead well one must follow the Chief Shepherd—the ultimate leader. Here Peter adopted the metaphor of Chief Shepherd to fit the present leadership context with the implication that these leaders are responsible to and take their cues from Christ the Chief Shepherd (Elliot, 2000). The shepherd metaphor is found consistently in this text for leaders and ties leadership not only to a certain style of leadership but that this leadership is done in imitation of Christ in His leadership as well. This can be seen as shown in Figure 5.

> **I Peter 5:1-6**
>
> a. 5:1 Personal imperative, Therefore – elders
>
> b. 5:2-3 Instruction to elders, shepherd the flock
>
> c. 5:4 Reward – crown of glory
>
> b' 5:5 Instruction to all, humble yourselves
>
> a' 5:6 Personal imperative, Therefore – humble yourselves

Figure 5: The chiastic structure of 1 Peter 5:1-6.

In the intertexture of this pericope, the power of the shepherd image recontextualized has already been discussed. However, this image is surrounded by other recontextualizations that are brought forward from the Old Testament in a very thick cultural texture surrounding the focus of leadership in this section. In addition, though elders are a concept from the Old Testament recontextualized for this setting, they also come from a social texture since elders come from the Greco-Roman world as well. The elders were modeled after the elders in Jewish tradition but they also existed throughout the Greco-Roman world (Elliot, 2000). First Peter 5:5b is a quotation of Proverbs 3:34 from the Septuagint, other than the substitution of "God" for "Lord," showing this exhortation to humility has the authority of Scripture and this humility expresses itself in the willingness to serve others beyond one's self-interest (Jobes, 2005). The expression of the "powerful hand of God" is used in the Old Testament for God disciplining His people in Ezekiel 20:34-35, but it is also an expression of deliverance in Exodus and Deuteronomy (Elliot, 2000). The instruction to cast all your anxiety on the Lord is an adaption of Psalm 54:23 (Elliot, 2000). The intertexture pictures of shepherd, elder, and flock, along with Old Testament exhortations concerning humility, create a thickly texture pericope filled with exhortation that is contemporary to the readers and pregnant with meaning from their cultural context. In addition, these cultural textures carry authority of Scripture as well as tradition even though they are recontextualized for the church since the church is the household of God.

Within this pericope is an important ideological texture concerning power. The leaders were told how to be shepherds as leaders in how they take oversight of the followers. Significantly, this section connects shepherding with the job of oversight and the tense indicates that it was something that needed to be done with ever new vigor, not out of routine, and then he expanded his explanation through three sets of contrasts (Davids, 1990). The job of the shepherd was to oversee the sheep but the leader was to do this in a certain way. Here the elders were to shepherd because they were overseers and this was probably a reference to Ezekiel 34:11 where the Lord promised to seek out the scattered sheep and oversee them (Jobes, 2005). This function of overseeing was related to the way God leads His people. The elders were to shepherd the flock by overseeing them as seen in three contrasting adverbial qualifiers (Jobes, 2005). These qualifiers explain how the elders are to use power as they shepherd the followers; they explain how they were to oversee. The perspective for leadership here was that the character of the leader was paramount as he qualified the exercise of oversight since their authorization as shepherds may call for them to exercise authority; it was authority with defined limits circumscribed by divine purpose and exemplified in Christ (Green, 2007). The three qualifiers are: (a) overseeing the people not as if forced, but willingly according to God; (b) overseeing them not greedy for gain but eager to be of service; and (c) overseeing them not as domineering but as role models or examples (Jobes, 2005). These three contrasts qualified the leadership of the elders in shepherding and their use of authority, in essence their use of the power of their position.

Peter gave the leaders instruction on how to oversee or lead as shepherds to the flock. His first instruction was to enter this place of leadership willingly, not under compulsion or by force. Elders were to be the shepherd over the flock eagerly or spontaneously not under compulsion (Witherington, 2007). Begrudging service was not to be a motivation for leadership as this will not be pleasing to God and leading should be done according in accordance with what is pleasing to God and this contrasts this oversight with the norms of Greco-Roman society

(Jobes, 2005). This leadership was affected by the motive to lead and was contrasted to societal leadership. This leadership was different in motive and pattern from other forms of leadership. The author qualified the exercise of oversight with the ideal spirit, proper motive, and appropriate manner of leadership (Elliot, 2000). Proper use of oversight was not only an issue of certain behaviors but also proper orientation in leadership or a proper spirit or attitude concerning why and how one leads.

The second part of the exhortation concerns not leading for greed or selfish gain. This was not talking about refusing money but instead was speaking of motive. Selfish interest was close at hand in all human hearts and especially in the work of leadership it must be constantly guarded against. This type of leadership was not for the promotion of self but for the fulfilling of the purpose of God which focused on the people not the needs of the leader. Leadership was not to be motivated by greed for financial gain but with an eagerness to serve others with a desire to give and not to get from others (Jobes, 2005). This qualification touches on motive and contrasts calculation with spontaneity elders should be motivated not by money but by an eagerness to give (Elliot, 2000). This is not only a contrast between money and service but also one of motive between a quest for personal gain and a quest to serve others.

Peter then contrasted becoming lords with becoming examples; this is a classic case of the process of humility. This term *domineering* can carry the meaning of harsh or excessive use of authority and Peter implied that it was not the use of force that should be used but that of example (Grudem, 1999). This was leadership by example, therefore it was imperative that the leader have a life worth following. Jesus was the perfect example but leaders were to live in such a way which others could imitate and this should not engender pride but instead humility (Grudem, 1999). This life of a leader proceeded from humility and leading others by example like they had been led by the example of Jesus the Chief Shepherd. This contrast was a warning against love of power; the leaders were not to be domineering but influence others as exemplars. This was not a hierarchical exercise of power but a horizontal demonstration by example (Elliot, 2000). This concept of leadership by example was common in the New Testament in following the pattern of the ancient world where leading was a matter of example rather than command (Davids, 1990). The leaders were to lead by example, from following the example of Christ; in addition, this was a leadership undergirded by humility and was the opposite of dominating leadership. It did not engender a hierarchy of power but a place of shared power with careful use of authority that was modified by proper motive and attitude in the leaders. Authority and power were moderated by internal issues of character that proceed from the inner person of the leader. This ontological aspect of the leader is then of paramount importance in proper effective leadership.

This section also asks the question of development. How can this ontology or character be developed in the leader and how were people like Peter developed as leaders? The answer to this is multifaceted. We saw in Chapter 4 that the inner person can be changed in the example of Sarah and Abraham. Up to this section of 1 Peter, suffering has been a major issue which was seen to bring change in perspective, attitude, and character with a proper response to it. What about practical training? Peter was trained by the example of Jesus which he now endorsed for his leaders. But was there more? Remember Peter used a certain form of rhetoric in this text, this had to be learned. In addition, this pericope brings out the extremely thick texture of connecting Old Testament Scriptures, pictures, and concepts to their contemporary predicament. This had to be learned and Peter now taught it to his hearers in 1 Peter. Leadership development can be seen as an issue of life development in ontological areas, as well as certain learned concepts of life, theology, philosophy, and communication. The inner texture of 1 Peter 5:1-7 can be seen in Table 13.

Table 13: Inner Texture of 1 Peter 5:1-7

Vs.	Repetitive	Progressive	Narrative
5.1	Elder (2x), glory	Elders-glory	Therefore I exhort—imperative
5:2	Shepherd, flock, God		Instruction to leaders
5:3	Flock		Instruction to leaders
5:4	Shepherd, glory	Shepherd-glory	Reward
5:5	Humble(2x), elder, God		Instruction to all
5:6	Humble, God	All-glory	Therefore, humble self-imperative

This section comes to a climax in its discussion of leadership. Leadership and leaders were addressed directly by Peter. The model for leadership was seen in the Chief Shepherd, as Jesus the ultimate leader, and other leaders were to follow and imitate Jesus not only in His suffering but also in His leadership. This leadership was collegial in that Peter the great apostle of the church considered himself a fellow elder with these leaders in the church. The many echoes and recontexualizations in this section show that leadership was to be patterned after God's leadership and to be done in accordance with His will and design. In this context, a key component of leadership was true humility, not self-degradation. In addition, it was found here that a proper attitude was needed for leadership in eager service and was in contradistinction to the leadership concepts of society. A proper motive was needed in a desire to give rather than a self-centered motive. A proper attitude toward authority and its use were also important in leadership in that authority was not for dominance but to lead by example just as one was to follow the example of Jesus Christ. Authority and power were moderated by internal issues of character and a proper sense of reality. It was also found that this type of leadership can be developed and one of the tools for this development was a proper response to suffering and humility under the mighty hand of God. The rich texture of Old Testament allusions, pictures, and reconfigurations set these concepts of leadership upon a foundation of theology and antiquity and these were also important elements in leadership development, in learning theology, and history. Leadership was an important issue in this text that surfaces full force in this pericope with examples, instructions, and clarifications about the use of power and authority.

1 Peter 5:8-14

This concluding pericope of the text continued with some final instructions before it gave the final salutations. A new section began here with an admonition of watchfulness. Peter warned his readers in a way that was similar to advising a person going down a dangerous road about being alert and careful because of the genuine danger of attacks by the enemy (Grudem, 1999). This final section was a warning concerning attacks of the enemy and how to meet this challenge. For Peter, the attack, which was mediated through people or persecutors, was coming from the devil or adversary from a word that originally meant an opponent in a lawsuit (Davids, 1990). The danger came from the devil but it manifested through the persecutions against believers by other people; it was spiritual but it manifested in the physical realm. Peter issued an urgent appeal while painting a vivid picture of the enemy urging firm resistance in the faith and concluding with encouragement (Hiebert, 1992). This vivid picture of the enemy was the backdrop to final instructions to the believers about suffering and how to respond.

In this short section, there is an inner texture with four repeated words: "suffer," "firm", "God," and "grace." These are connected in this repetitive texture in their message about responding to the enemy. In addition, there is a thick sacred texture in discussion about deity or God, a spirit being or the devil, and human commitment to God. These textures are tightly woven together in this short section bringing important understandings to light concerning suffering and proper human response as well as the ultimate results.

Each of the terms in the repetitive texture here—"suffer," "firm," "grace," and "God"—are mentioned twice in this short section. In addition, "grace" and "God" are only mentioned together while "suffer" and "firm" concern the human side of this battle with the adversary. This word for firm is used for solid objects, meaning hard, but is used figuratively here of humans and their character; it could even mean stubborn or firmness in respect to their faith (Elliot, 2000). Firm faith is a remedy for attacks from the enemy or a firm perseverance in the face of opposition. Firm faith is the way to resist the attacks of the devil. The word "resist" implies active determined opposition and it is to the attacks of the devil which can be the cause of some of the suffering (Grudem, 1999). The attacks of the devil come as suffering but these attacks can be defeated by resistance that is being solid, even stubborn in faith, even in the face of opposition. The believers are also exhorted to stand firm in the grace of God as well. The believers must now live in and through this grace as the graced people of God; the challenge is to stand fast in the divine grace that shapes their past, present, and future, and the intention of this exhortation was to reassure them in suffering of God's sustaining grace and to motivate them to an honorable way of life in their identity as the household of God (Elliot, 2000). They were to stand firm in faith and grace in resisting the enemy in the context of suffering.

Suffering is also mentioned twice here but in close proximity in the text. It was important for them to know that others were suffering in the same way. In 1 Peter 5:9, the verb has the sense of being completed and suggested the implication that God was the ultimate source, and perhaps meaning that suffering was being brought to its completion or goal which was not destruction but its opposite, purification and glorification (Witherington, 2007). Here the verb connoted "causing something to happen as fulfillment of a purpose," in other words suffering was not meaningless. In this, Peter rejected the idea that the devil can create havoc in a way that would threaten God's sovereignty; these trials serve God's purpose of testing (Green, 2007). Suffering was in the sovereign will of God though it may be brought by the devil who the believer was to resist, but at the same time suffering worked purification. This suffering, however, would be brief and would be concluded with strengthening from God (Elliot, 2000). Although Peter acknowledged the inevitability of Christian suffering, he also affirmed the relative brevity of it and though it could be that it was brief and sporadic, it is more likely that he was saying that in the light of eternal glory, the lifetime in this body with the potential for suffering was but a little while (Jobes, 2005). This suffering was a part of this mortal life and though it could come at different points in life, the result is both strengthening and glory.

Glory is an important word in this texture as well. It is mentioned two other times in this chapter previous to this section. Throughout the letter, Peter used the word "glory" to refer to the state of being that was accomplished by the sufferings and resurrection of Christ, to be fully revealed at His return and which new life in Christ is even now a part and this new realm of being is eternal, making suffering here but fleeting (Jobes, 2005). Glory is then a state of being that is present yet will only be fully revealed in eternity and in this new reality even suffering is temporary though fully present for the moment. Peter spoke of partaking of this glory now and future and this same glory is available to all who have entered this new reality of the resurrection of Christ.

The two words in the repetitive structure are "grace" and "God" which are both mentioned together both times in this pericope. The first time, it is the God of grace that calls into glory after suffering and the second time it is standing firm in the grace of God in the midst of the suffering. The God of all grace is characterizing God in the most fundamental way as the God whose grace is sufficient for every type of situation and His character is love and concern for the welfare of His people even in their suffering with the intention that they should share in His glory (Marshall, 1991). In the midst of suffering God gives grace, since He is the God of all grace. This grace is sufficient for the challenge of the suffering to bring His people through into glory, into victory, into this new reality. This grace or the generous favor of God in 5:10 and 5:12 summarizes in one word the letter's witness as a whole and it stresses the divine call of believers into glory (Elliot, 2000). God gives favor and grace to the believers in the midst of suffering as He strengthens them and brings them into this new reality of glory. Peter declared in Verse 12 that this is the true grace of God referring to the total experience described in this letter and the readers should stand fast in this testimony (Marshall, 1991). In this statement about the grace of God is found the intention of this letter to give eschatological perspective to their suffering, to point out the grace of God they would receive and were receiving to encourage them to continue in trust in God (Davids, 1990). The God of all grace gives divine grace to His people in the midst of their troubles and suffering to help them walk through these sufferings and receive glory, present, and future.

There is a rich sacred texture here in this final pericope of this document. The texture centers around three important aspects of sacred texture: (a) deity or God, (b) a spirit being or the devil in this instance, and (c) human commitment in resisting this spirit being and continuing in commitment to God. In this section, God is seen in relationship to grace and glory. However, He is also seen as the initiator of strength to those who are firm in suffering. Peter used four nearly synonymous verbs to describe what God would do for the benefit of the faithful believers after some time has passed in that God will put things right, strengthen, empower, and secure them (Jobes, 2005). These are the actions of God in and for the believer who has been faithful, standing firm in the faith in suffering. The focus is on God that God will fortify the community with four actions that are manifestations of God's grace (Elliot, 2000). God is active on behalf of those who have stood firm. The word for "complete" includes putting in order or make whole or complete; God will make the believers whole (Elliot, 2000). The focus is on their character in that through their suffering God will produce a fully restored character in them (Davids, 1990). The second verb is a future tense word meaning to fix firmly or to establish, most frequently used to mean reinforce or strengthen especially in adversity (Elliot). This is used in the sense of causing one to become more firm and unchanging in attitude of belief (Jobes, 2005). The third verb is a future from of the word meaning to strengthen or fill with strength and it overlaps in meaning with the previous word (Elliot, 2000). God Himself will empower the believer (Jobes, 2005). Finally, God will "settle them," meaning to place on a foundation and this is an image of security (Davids, 1990). God will establish the believers so that their defenses will rest on a firm foundation and not be undermined (Marshall, 1991). These four terms are closely related terms that together reinforce one another and underscore the good that God is intending for them and is now producing in their suffering (Davids, 1990). The result of perseverance in suffering is a divine grace that will provide new strength, wholeness, peace, and firmness in their foundations. These results come from an external source—from God—but they affect the community of believers in their character and their internal issues of security and peace.

The second aspect of the sacred texture is that of a spirit being named in this section which is the devil. He is described in this section as well as his operation in opposing believers. The term used for Satan here has the root meaning of slanderer or accuser or even tempter and Peter was connecting the assault of Satan with physical suffering of some of the believers (Witherington, 2007). Satan is described further as an adversary, which is an opponent or enemy (Davids, 1990). The devil refers to a spiritual being who is in active rebellion against God and who has the ability and the propensity to attack Christians (Grudem, 1999). This spirit being is responsible at least in part for some of this suffering among the believers as their adversary.

He is then described as a lion who is roaring, prowling, and seeking to devour. This comparison of the devil to a lion communicates the enemy's deadly ferocity and devouring capacity in keeping with the image of a shepherd and sheep as one who is the enemy of the flock and a very powerful one as well (Elliot, 2000). The term "devour" is a graphic term meaning to "drink down" and it pictures the destruction of the believer which is the desire of Satan (Davids, 1990). This desire and ability of the devil to destroy is cause for a response from the believer.

The final sacred texture concerns human commitment to God in response to this design of the enemy through suffering. In response to this lion-like activity of the enemy, the believer is to be alert and sober while resisting the devil in standing firm in the faith. This human commitment to God in the midst of the battle against the enemy in suffering after some time brings divine actions of grace. The first verb "be sober" is avoiding the effects of intoxication and the second refers to shaking off the effects of sleep, and both words in the Greek language end exactly alike, creating a memorable rhetorical effect (Witherington, 2007). The emphasis is on one's focus of attention and is the opposite of drowsiness in which one sees and responds to situations no differently than unbelievers without God's perspective (Grudem, 1999). This intense warning is to pay attention to what is really happening and to see from God's perspective so as not to be deceived in responding in the normal way to suffering or attacks of the enemy. The encouragement to resist him and stand firm in faith implies a confidence that God will intervene and give victory not defeat and they will grow in faith and God will take Satan's plans for evil and turn them to good (Grudem, 1999). Here resistance is linked to being strong in faith denoting something firmly established (Witherington, 2007). Response to the devil is two-fold in being alert, viewing issues from God's perspective, and resisting the devil by being strongly founded in faith. Resisting is not resolving the suffering, it is seeing that the suffering is a work of the oppose to destroy the believer and in reality it is part of the purpose of God in purifying, strengthening, and settling the believer as they pass through the test by the grace of God. These textures can be seen in Table 14.

Table 14: Inner and Sacred Texture of 1 Peter 5:8-14

Vs.	Repetitive	Deity	Spirit being	Human commitment
5:8			Devil, adversary, lion, devour	Sober, alert
5:9	Suffer, firm			Resist, firm, suffer
5:10	Suffer, God, Grace	God, grace, glory, perfect, establish, strengthen, confirm		
5:11				
5:12	God, grace			
5:13				
5:14				

In this section is seen the importance of suffering not as something to be tolerated but received and seen properly. For it is in a proper response to suffering that strength, wholeness, and foundations are established that are important to leaders and leadership. In this context, there is instruction to pay close attention to that which occurs around a person and to see from a new perspective, a divine one. This new perspective arms one with proper insights to stand firm in suffering and receive the reward of glory which is a new reality both present and future. This proper response to suffering effects and brings positive to change to the character of the person on an ontological level. These tests though in a certain sense are from the enemy, they ultimately come from God for the process of change in the believer in character, for the sake of walking in glory and grace. The key here is perseverance in suffering or a fierce resolve to press through the suffering, trouble, or disaster to live in the glory and grace, to pass the test and receive the strength and internal change that God is doing.

Be shepherds of God's flock that is under your care, serving as overseers.
Peter, NASB

CHAPTER 14

I PETER – THE BIG PICTURE

1 Peter 1:1 – 5:18
In the context of the complete document, there are textures that come to the surface in this study. There are several that have already been mentioned since they show up repeatedly in the separate pericopes of this text. Among them are the picture of the shepherd as leader and the concept of suffering resulting in change and growth. In addition, this text has a thick intertexture with the Old Testament not only in Old Testament pictures like that of shepherd but also Scriptures that are recontextualized for the new setting in the New Testament household of God.

Historical intertexture asks the question of the events that occurred in this text whether there can be corroborating evidence of the events as stated in the text (Robbins, 1996). Can the suffering in the text of 1 Peter among the believers be corroborated with historical data and were these general difficulties or threats of martyrdom? It is impossible to place the historical situation of 1 Peter with the persecution under Nero or any other emperor, but the presence of unofficial harassment by the populace is easier to see here and the situation in 1 Peter of suffering by believers is easy to place throughout the Roman Empire and therefore difficult to pinpoint on a timeline (Green, 2007). It is possible to place this document in the 1st-century Roman Empire with its general persecution against Christians while it is difficult to know the exact time of the text. Nevertheless, the 1st-century Roman Empire could very likely be the backdrop to this text. A redaction of 1 Peter led to the belief that 1 Peter was written during the time of the writings of Trajan (A.D. 109-111), but the character of the persecution referred to throughout the book seems limited to verbal slander, malicious talk, and false accusations reflecting an earlier time than indicated by Trajan's writings (Jobes, 2005). The historical setting is likely in the 1st century when there were generalized oppositions to the church. This would indicate that the claim of the text to be written by Peter the apostle is true. It appears that 1 Peter does indeed come from Simon bar Jonah the follower of Jesus near the end of his life in the late 60s (Witherington, 2009b). This historical intertexture aligns with the claims of the text or Petrine authorship and in the context of suffering in the early years of the church.

The social and cultural texture addresses the social and cultural nature of the text searching out the kind of person that lives in the world of the text (Robbins, 1996). Specific social topics discuss certain ways of talking about the world and different responses create a different culture (Robbins, 1996). In the text of 1 Peter is found the thaumaturgic response to the world in the context of suffering. The thaumaturgical response is that culture or type of response that focuses on the concerns of individual people for relief for present ills (Robbins, 1994). First Peter has a focus of dealing with present suffering but with a surprising answer, of a new reality of the present *eschaton*, however, it still concerns a response to the present ills. This response becomes part of the culture of the readers of 1 Peter and the household of God but it is not one of withdrawal, it is one of engagement, but in a new even surprising way. This letter cannot be read in terms of resistance to or withdrawal from society but instead from the purpose of its primary orientation, the end, or the actualization of God's purpose in believers following the Christ who suffered as well (Green, 2007). This response to suffering is practical and paradoxical which brings us to the next social response in this document.

Most historical manifestations of religious communities exhibit a relationship of two or three types of responses to the world (Robbins, 2004). The way the problems are addressed are through the transformation of perspective, reality, and of one's inner person or character. It is neither resistance nor intense optimism about those causing the trouble. This Gnostic response is also seen in the leadership issues brought to the forefront in 1 Peter. The Gnostic response believes that transformed relationships are needed and that salvation is possible if people learn the right means to address problems (Robbins, 2004). Salvation here is not just spiritual redemption, it is also in the sense of deliverance or healing. Deliverance or wholeness come through learning the right ways to address suffering and the need is transformed relationships with the Lord particularly but also in unique transformed relationships between leader and follower. The relationship is not one of power but is transformed and is one of care in the tradition of the shepherd.

Final cultural categories of rhetoric are those topics that most decisively identify one's cultural location whether it is dominant, subculture, counterculture, contraculture, or luminal (Robbins, 1996). In this document is found countercultural rhetoric in Peter and the readers responding to a dominant culture and projecting a new future. Counter culture rhetoric evokes a new future with insights for alternative minicultures making provisions for men and women in differing age groups and this culture develops appropriate institutions to sustain the group (Roberts, 1978). First Peter develops these instructions to different groups in addressing the dominant culture and building new institutions as the household of God with countercultural leadership styles.

In these textures, leadership is seen as countercultural based on transformed relationships, not based in the social norms. It comes through learning the proper way of dealing with suffering and with power. This document challenges leaders to lead in a new way that is set by the example of Christ and based on the model of a shepherd. In addition, leadership focuses on helping people with suffering by focusing on the actualization of God's purpose in the transformation of the person rather than the immediate problem. The whole concept is not just countercultural to a particular culture, it is countercultural to the general human culture.

The Big Picture Principles

The text of 1 Peter has been examined closely for data concerning principles of leadership using socio-rhetorical interpretation. This examination brought several principles to the surface concerning the teaching of this text about leadership. These principles were shown in several forms including direct address, recontextualized cultural concepts, examples, and exhortations. The context was Peter's instruction for the community or the household of faith in several geographic locations. These principles were repeated and reinforced from different aspects in this document.

God is the foundation of all things according to this text and this includes power. Power properly comes to individuals through a progressive process of refinement. The person in this process is transformed through a process of suffering and responding to God. In this context, suffering is reconfigured from an issue of judgment to an issue of transformation. This transformation is an internal work in the soul of the person. In addition, this leadership is seen in Peter who leads through instruction and vision to the community but as one who has been transformed.

This internal preparation or transformation involves the mind, the will, and the being of the person. Holiness is reconfigured from an external issue to an internal one and this transformation process changes the person ontologically. It is a change in the inner person. The person is to be holy in imitation of the Lord and this change is ontological and this imitation is a mimesis of the Lord Himself. Though the change is internal it affects behavior. Ontologically, a new reality is constructed for the people here as well a new reality based on the resurrection of Jesus Christ from the dead and a new reality in that now the community is a community of priests. He leads this community of priests in defining their real identity and then ultimate reality as well. Leadership comes from transformation in the being of the person as well as his or her identity and understanding reality as well as leading others in defining and living in ultimate reality. However, this is done in mimesis of the Lord in His suffering or change process and His leadership.

Leadership includes the idea of suffering and submission without grasping for authority following the example of Christ the overseer and shepherd. In this, the leader is to follow very closely the example of Christ or, in mimesis, follow the Lord as overseer (one who guides) and a shepherd (one who cares) and to lead by example. Leadership is giving guidance, providing care, and setting the example or the model for others to follow. To do this, an individual must develop inner character through transformation and responding well to opposition trouble, slander, and false accusations. This way of leading with authority that is caring, guiding, and in imitation of Christ is in contradistinction to the cultural norms of authority that are reward and punishment driven. In this way of leadership, the suffering servant becomes the ultimate leader and sets the example of leadership. Leadership is in imitation of this suffering servant shepherd and overseer.

A leader is also to be a steward, one who is in charge of the household but as a faithful servant, not as an owner. This faithful servant is faithful and effective in the use of the gifts that have been given to them. They use these gifts in service to the community or the others that they lead. This servant sees suffering as part of the growth process to become more effective as servant and leader and this process changes not only the inner person and the understanding of reality it also changes one's perception. This perception change affects the ethics and values of the person as well. In this, the person learns to use power well and properly like God uses power. God uses power paradoxically using weakness to show strength and using humility to express true power.

Leaders are tested and need to be tested to do well in the test bringing purification, strength, and joy. Understanding and embracing suffering is an important source of character development. These internal characteristics are a source of strength and effectiveness for leadership. They help develop the leader ontologically in integrity and trust which are needed for leadership. In addition, this attitude toward suffering and testing is an imitation of mimesis of Christ in His suffering as well. However, in the midst of this testing and purification the leader must have a proper vision of the future to have a proper perspective for the present in leading others.

This leader as the Shepherd is to imitate the Chief Shepherd in suffering and leadership patterned after the leadership of God, not after the norms of society. The leader is to provide eager service rather than out of obligation. The leader is to have a proper motive in leading in desiring to give rather than to get something. The leader is to have a proper attitude toward authority, not using it for domination but instead to set the role model or the example for others to follow like they follow the suffering servant shepherd leader. The leader uses power and authority properly since they are moderated by the internal issues of good character and a proper sense of reality based on the glory and the will of God. Leadership involves true humility that is not self-degradation. This humility is the source of exaltation and true power. The issues of leadership transcend the issues of self and personal desire. This type of leadership is developed in a proper response to suffering and humility under the work of God. This should be done in the context of developing a proper understanding of theology and antiquity or history.

In the proper response to suffering strength and wholeness is developed along with a new perspective. In addition, there is a new ability to stand firm and to stand or move into the future with a fierce resolve. Perseverance in this suffering brings the reward of glory which is a new reality both present and future. This standing firm facilitates not only a new reality but the ability to fulfill ones purpose in living out the will of God. This internal change that is worked in the person produces resolve, perseverance, and character for walking in this new reality. The leader is then able to lead others into this new reality helping them develop strength and good character.

Leadership is countercultural not just to specific cultures, but to the human culture or cultures in general. It is based on transformed people and relationships, not on social norms. This leadership is based upon learning the proper way of dealing with suffering and power in following the example of Christ in serving, suffering, and leading as a shepherd. Effective leaders then help others with suffering and working out the purpose of God for their lives in facilitating transformation of the followers and society as well.

These 17 findings in the text of 1 Peter can be seen as several distinct principles, however, they are related and connected to each other forming a style of leadership. These issues of leadership connect with each other in formative ways in that transformation brings ontological change which brings a new identity and a new reality to the person who in this process develops humility, perseverance, purpose, and vision, as well as the ability to help others develop these concepts in their lives. At its root, the process is mimetic in imitation of Christ and the leader is to provide an example for others to follow. In other words, in imitating Christ, leaders provide an example for others to follow in following them like they follow Christ. This mimesis permeates this style of leadership. A summary of the findings in First Peter for leadership are detailed in the following list: (a) process of power through suffering reconfigured for transformation, (b) leadership is ontological in a change in the inner being and a new reality, (c) leadership is mimetic in an imitation of God and Christ as suffering shepherd, overseer, servant, (d) leadership is constructing reality and new self-identity in others, (e) lead through using authority in caring and guiding, not in reward and punishment, (f) steward as leader in proper use of gifts in serving community and using power paradoxically, (g) leading through a changed perspective affecting ethics, values and behavior, (h) testing brings new identity, purification, strength, and joy, (i) understanding suffering brings issues of integrity and trust, (j) vision needed to see the future to have a proper perspective for the present, (k) leadership development through response to suffering, humility, theology, history, (l) leaders walk in new reality both present and future, (m) leaders have strength for perseverance and fierce resolve, (n) leadership is countercultural based on transformation of relationships and society, (o) leaders help others with suffering through transformation of the person, (p) leaders live in purpose or destiny and call and help others find and live in their purpose, and (q) humility is an integral part of leadership in leading and leadership development.

Mimesis also provides a pattern for leadership development. This development process for the principles of 1 Peter involves learning to deal appropriately with suffering and develop internal issues like humility. These issues are important not only for leaders but for all believers. The leaders develop these qualities in the imitation of Christ in His suffering and how He suffered as well as His humility and attitude. People and leaders are trained by following others who have learned these life and leadership lessons. Leadership is not only mimetic, followership is mimetic and the training for followers and leaders is through imitation. This is confirmed by other pericopes of the New Testament in which Paul said to follow him as he followed the Lord in 1 Corinthians 11:1. The writer of the book of Hebrews said in 13:7 that the believers should call to memory their leaders and imitate them. Spener desired to reform the church in the 17th century through reformed education of church leaders—through education by teachers setting the example of living the gospel and its results laying stress on pious lives (Richard, 1897). The leaders would train other leaders by example. The teachers would accomplish a great deal by their example and the students would realize that they must live as examples for the flock (Spener, 1964). The students would be trained by example to be examples and these examples were the teachers or leaders who followed Christ. These concepts from Peter are connected in bringing important change to the one who leads ontologically in following Christ, who are then those who lead by setting the example for others. These leaders are developed through the transformations as shown in the text of 1 Peter in following Christ and even Peter in his following of Christ as a fellow elder with the other leaders. The leadership itself is mimetic as well as the process of learning and developing leadership. These concepts are related and can be formed into principles from the text and teaching of 1 Peter.

Perhaps this letter's universal relevance is due to its presentation of how the gospel of Jesus Christ is the foundational principle by which the Christian life is lived out within the larger unbelieving society.
Karen Jobes

CHAPTER 15

PRINCIPLES FROM PETER

In the beginning of this study, the question was asked concerning what kind of practices were developed by Peter in the text of 1 Peter and whether these principles or practices and style of leadership support or negate the contemporary models of leadership in authentic or kenotic leadership. In this text, Peter wrote to the Christian community regarding several issues concerning suffering, authority, and countercultural practices that were important for the believers. This document is an ad hoc pastoral document and even the theological discussions serve as the undergirding for the ethics, values, virtues, and practices being inculcated by the author who was constructing the ethos of the community under fire and the counsel about rulers, elders, and others was the outworking of the theology and ideology of the author (Witherington, 2007). This outworking becomes principles for leadership that can be drawn from this text.

Peter reoriented and reconfigured reality around the purposes of God and invited the reader to see from God's perspective in several areas including suffering and leadership. First Peter is about God and the ramifications of orienting life around Him, including rejection of the conventions of honor and status in Roman society in favor of the ways of God whose ways are countercultural to the Roman system and it is an invitation to adopt God's way of seeing things and into a lifestyle of formation in the character and ways of God (Green, 2007). This invitation is not just to a way of thinking, it is to a way of being as well as living. The relationship between the Christian and culture is the overarching theme of this text, in that Peter encouraged a transformed understanding of self-identity that redefined how one is to live and these principles of Peter's differentiated acceptance and rejection of culture offer the letter's most significant contribution to the thought of its time (Jobes, 2005). It is in this context of the discussion of culture and a transformed self-identity that leadership is discussed and reconfigured in 1 Peter in contrast to leadership in Roman culture. First Peter is a significant work of New Testament theology and pastoral care with a concern for the community and leaders and the author identified himself as a fellow leader among them (Davids, 1990). This concern for pastoral care is seen in Peter as the leader as well as his concerns for the leaders to whom he wrote. Peter called himself an apostle and it was apostles who gave guidance on choosing leaders and yet he was a fellow elder as well following the example of the Chief Shepherd, Jesus Christ (Witherington, 2007). Peter gave instruction for leaders in following the example of Christ which he was endeavoring to do as well in leading them and guiding them in their leadership as an apostle who was directing them about the kind of people who were to be leaders in the community.

Leadership Principles in 1 Peter

From this examination there were found 17 aspects or instructions that are important to leadership. These seventeen aspects can be seen as ten principles drawn from 1 Peter for leadership. These ten principles can be seen in the following list (a) transformation through suffering – power, identity, integrity, trust, (b) ontological change in inner person, reality, perspective, (c) leadership is mimetic – imitation of Christ as shepherd, overseer, servant, (d) proper use of authority, (e) steward leadership – proper use of gifts and power, (f) vision to see the future and the present, (g) strength for perseverance and fierce resolve, (h) live in purpose and destiny, (i) humility is an integral aspect of leadership, and (j) Leadership development through proper response to suffering, then humility, theology, and history.

Principle 1: Transformation Through Suffering

The text of 1 Peter focuses on suffering and it is in this context that the several issues of leadership, community, and transformation are discussed. The purpose of 1 Peter is to encourage the readers to grow in their trust in God and their obedience to him especially when they suffer (Grudem, 1999). The reason that Peter wrote this document was to show the appropriate Christian response to suffering (Seagraves, 2010). In this context, suffering is reconfigured from the result of evil to a process of refining the person as the person is transformed by proper response to suffering and to God wherein power is progressively given to him or her in this transformation process. Transformation is seen as a key issue in contemporary leadership but normally it has to do with the leader transforming and motivating the followers for the sake of the organization (Bass, 1990; Yukl, 2002). Nevertheless, in this context, it has to do with transformation in the leader first before any transformation takes place in others or society. This transformation takes place through a proper response to suffering and trouble. The core of character is normally formed best in the crucible of testing (Guinness, 2000). It is not a question of whether suffering and trouble happens but how one responds when it does happen. It is this response in faith and hope that brings transformation. Suffering is paradoxical in that though it appears to bring negative things it is just the opposite and in this testing of suffering brings a new identity in Christ, as well as purification, strength, and joy. The fruit of joy is a wonderful characteristic for a leader because no matter what the challenges, joy will give the leader the inner confidence required to remain calm and give the leader strength under pressure (M. K. Collins, 2006).

In responding properly to suffering, leaders develop integrity and trust which are important ingredients for leadership. Leaders build trust and act with integrity (Kouzes & Posner, 2007). Ethics needs to be at the heart of leadership and leadership studies with ethical values such as honesty, integrity, and trustworthiness (Ciulla, 2004). These ingredients, while considered important in leadership, ask the question of the source of these qualities. Is one simply born with these valuable assets for leadership? Part of the answer is found in 1 Peter in a proper response to suffering and understanding that suffering is a test not to judge but to build one's inner person. Then leaders help followers through their suffering and transformation as well by setting the example for them. This aspect of leadership is countercultural based on transformation of the person transforming relationships and even society. These relationships are not based upon power but upon transformed relationships between leader and follower.

Principle 2: Ontological Change

Closely related to transformation is the need for ontological change or change in one's being and perspective of reality. The power of leadership transformation begins with the heart of the person where godly character is created in the leader and becomes evident in his or her life as it starts in the inner person and then produces good fruit (M. K. Collins, 2006). The preparation for leadership is internal involving the mind, the will, and the very being of the individual in imitation of God in holiness, but it is reconfigured holiness from an external issue to an internal one. However, this is ontological in two ways with the first being growth and change in one's inner being. The second has to do with understanding ultimate reality and reconstructing reality. Leaders energize followers by creating meaning and positively constructing reality for themselves and their followers (Avolio et al., 2004). Peter was reconstructing reality for the community of priests in this text, redefining their self-identity and showing a new reality. In this context, suffering is relevant in that it is here that suffering changes one's perception of reality. This understanding and embracing suffering can be a source for character and leadership development. This changed perspective results in changed behavior particularly in the area of ethics and values. Values influence every aspect of our lives, our judgments, responses, and commitments; they serve as guides to actions and inform decisions (Kouzes & Posner, 2007). Then leaders walk in this new reality both present and for the future.

Principle 3: Leadership is Mimetic

We have already seen that leadership involves an imitation of God in holiness in the ontological aspect of leadership. However, there is a further sense to this mimesis in this text. The leader is to imitate God in His leadership as seen in Christ as the shepherd, overseer, and servant. Jesus Christ is the Chief Shepherd and there are specific ways that He is to be imitated. First, He is to be imitated in His suffering. The essence of ancient education was following good models or imitating them and the idea here is the patient endurance of unjust suffering with Christ as the model, following His pattern (Witherington, 2007). Then in this context, Christ is held up as the leader, as a shepherd, and an overseer, and with an exhortation to use freedom in this new reality to serve. The example here of Christ is the suffering servant, overseer, and shepherd. In this model of shepherd leadership, Peter gave three contrasts. The shepherd is to oversee the flock of God willingly in accord with God, not as one compelled, eagerly and not for gain, by being an example to the flock and not domineering (Elliott, 2000). They must not lead by force or begrudgingly which has to do with the proper attitude in leading. This type of leadership is not for the promotion of self and speaks of the motive of giving in leadership rather than getting from others. Then, finally, this type of leadership is done by example or being the role model rather than as an overlord or domineering power figure. Jesus is the perfect example but leaders are to live in such a way that others could imitate as well (Grudem, 1999). Kenotic leadership is mimetic in following Christ in emptying Himself which leaders are to follow (Bekker, 2007b). In addition, Kouzes and Posner (2007) saw a key component of leadership as providing a role model for others to follow. This shepherd leadership is following the example of Christ in leading, in attitude, and motive so as to set the example for others to follow.

Principle 4: Proper Use of Authority

The leader is to use authority properly in caring and guiding, not through reward and punishment. Authority involves the rights, duties, and obligations associated with a particular position and it involves the right to exercise control or power and success depends greatly on the manner in which this power is exercised, whether subtle and careful or arrogant and domineering (Yukl, 2002). Authority and power in 1 Peter are moderated by internal issues of character and a proper sense of reality. A proper attitude toward authority and its use are important here for leadership in that authority is not for dominance but to be able to lead by example. Effective leaders use power carefully and, in contrast, those who use it arrogantly or manipulatively are likely to engender resistance to their leadership (Yukl, 2002).

Principle 5: Steward Leadership

A steward leader is one who leads as a servant in charge of another's goods. This steward is not an owner, but as a servant is a fellow servant with others in accomplishing certain goals together with others. A steward leader is to properly use the gifts that have been given them and be careful to use power properly, not just carefully as in the last section but paradoxically. These gifts of grace of speaking or serving are to be used for the community and not for the status of the individual leader. In the past, certain traits were considered important to leadership like strong verbal ability and further a leader-centered concept with a focus on skills that could be learned and developed was part of leadership approaches for effective leaders (Northouse, 2004). However, gifts as seen in 1 Peter are more than traits or skills. They are gifts given in speaking or serving that can be developed but need to be used in leading and developing the community not for personal gain. These are not to develop the status or the honor of the person but they are to bring glory to God. This divesting of prestige and power, as found in the kenosis of Christ, inherent in the leadership transaction, allows the leader and follower to have a new relationship that is marked with equality and service (Bekker, 2007b). This equality and service are aspects of steward leadership.

In addition, in light of the *eschaton* or the end of the age, the leader is not only to have a steward mentality concerning his or her gifts and their use, the leader is also to use power carefully. This use of power is in imitation of God who uses His power paradoxically. To bring redemption, God uses His power through the suffering of Jesus and He uses His power to change people in the midst of suffering. Luther called this the theology of the cross in God revealing His power through weakness rather than a display of divine will and fortitude (Althaus, 1966). The leader must learn to use power paradoxically in imitation of God using power to bring glory to God and to reveal His character rather than as a source of human will and desire.

Principle 6: Vision for the Future

The leader needs to be able to see the future clearly for proper perspective in the present. As the leader, Peter was giving his readers instruction and vision for a plan for the extension of God's work. Peter was concerned that the community would see the future properly to give true perspective of the present, and therefore a proper vision of the future and how it influences the present is a key ingredient for leaders. Developing a strong vision that can be communicated to followers is a key ingredient in transformational leadership (Bass, 1990; Yukl, 2002) and other forms of leadership (Kouzes & Posner, 2007). Not only is the future possible to anticipate, but also the way to think about the future as a sequence of events that can be influenced by personal choice and design may be one of the most powerful forces in one's life (Canton, 2007). Seeing the future is important to leadership for the present. Peter wanted the leaders to see the present in light of the future tests to come. Vision not only helps to shape the present it also helps to influence the future.

Principle 7: Perseverance

Leaders need strength to persevere with fierce resolve in difficult situations. The proper response to suffering is perseverance and faith and the key is fierce resolve to press through whatever trouble or situation presents itself to be able to walk in the glory and grace of God. The result of perseverance in suffering is a divine grace that will provide new strength, wholeness, peace, and firmness. The text in Peter uses several nearly synonymous verbs to describe what God will do for the benefit of the believers after some time has passed in persevering in suffering, He will strengthen, empower, and secure the person (Jobes, 2005). According to J. Collins (2001), one of the two important ingredients for great leaders is a fierce resolve even in the midst of adverse situations. This fierce resolve is a component of leadership concepts found in 1 Peter.

Principle 8: Living in Purpose

A leader needs to live in the purpose of God or their call and destiny, and help others find and live in their purpose as well. Standing firm in suffering facilitates not only perseverance but also the ability to live out one's purpose or destiny. Peter's own call to ministry was mentioned in this text both in the first verse of the text and his call as a fellow elder with the other leaders. Those who successfully follow the Lord must learn to live for the will of God for a higher purpose and even arm themselves with the mentality of suffering as part of the process. One can choose either to live in the flesh in the sense of this human existence for human desires or for the will of God (Davids, 1990). Calling is for everyone, everywhere, and life purpose comes from two areas: what we were created to be and what we are called to be and this call is the source of the deepest self-discoveries and growth in life it gives life and inspiration and a dynamism (Guinness, 2003). This purpose is important for leaders to discover like Moses, David, Peter, and Paul did, but it is also important to help others find this as well as the readers of 1 Peter are exhorted to be able to live according to the will of God.

Principle 9: Humility

Humility is an integral part of leadership as declared by Peter to the leaders of the community to whom this document was written. A key component of leadership is true humility not self-degradation. Humility is part of the essence in what it means to be like Christ and Peter told the leaders they were to model this virtue following the lead of the Chief Shepherd and the Lord would give them grace to continue in humility and service (Witherington, 2007). Humility is an integral component of effective leadership and leaders not only lead with humility they also teach humility by example which is important to followership and to life itself. All leadership and followership is to be done in the context of serving one another and leadership is seen as a form of service in humility (Witherington). Leadership is not about position and power but humility and service that proceeds from the character of the person. One's character lies deeper than philosophies, a person's character expresses most deeply what constitutes him or her as a unique individual (Guinness, 2000). Humility is not a behavior but characteristics that proceed from ones inner person who has developed humility. Positional authority and humility should not be mutually exclusive in that the two may coexist in the character of the leader (Ayers, 2006). J. Collins (2001), after extensive research, declared that deep personal humility is one of the two key ingredients for leaders to become great leaders.

This humility includes humility toward others, followers, and peers as well as humility under the hand of God. Humility at its core has to do with being aware that we are creatures and not the lords of our own lives in that we live under the authority and reality of God (Witherington, 2007). This life under the hand of God is part of the reality in which the leader lives and invites others into in the state of humility. Humility, in its purest form is actually the greatest source of personal power and, according to Benedict of Nursia, humility is the key to true leadership above all other marks of character (Galbraith & Galbraith, 2004). Humility is a key foundational component to leadership and in the imitation of Christ in His leadership.

Principle 10: Leadership Development

Leadership development is a process of learning to properly

respond to suffering, then a development of humility and an understanding of theology and history. This type of leadership can be developed and one of the tools for this process is a proper response to suffering and humility under the mighty hand of God. The entire text is about learning to respond properly to suffering and to understand this new concept of suffering recontextualized as the process of inner change. The goal of going through these trials is not destruction but its opposite purification (Witherington, 2007). The ultimate exhortation here is to be clothed with humility. The picture is putting on clothing like an apron for a slave (Jobes, 2005). This humility is developed in the person as something to put on like personal clothing. These aspects would be developed in the form of ancient education of imitation. In addition, the rich texture of Old and New Testament allusions, pictures, and reconfigurations set these concepts of leadership upon a foundation of the theology of Scripture in addition to the cultural pictures of Judaism and the Greco-Roman world or history. Leadership development in these principles should then include an understanding of history and theology particularly in these issues that are deeply embedded in this text.

These ten principles then constitute a concept of leadership as seen and developed by Peter in the context of the community of believers in this time period. These concepts of leadership have relevance for us as well in our context since these same principles that applied to human experience are still applicable. These principles can be compared to contemporary models of leadership and then be examined for their ramifications for ecclesial leadership as well as organizational leadership.

> The relationship between the Christian and culture is an overarching theme of 1 Peter, as relevant now as it was when first penned.
> Karen Jobes

CHAPTER 16

PETER IN CONTEMPORARY CONTEXT

A contemporary model of leadership that is growing in popularity as well as in research is authentic leadership. Authentic leadership as a contemporary model of leadership has spiritual components as well as certain ontological elements for leadership. Nevertheless, when compared to the principles as found in the text of 1 Peter the question is whether these two constructs are similar or different. According to Klenke (2007), authentic leadership has three identity systems: self-identity, leadership–identity and spiritual–identity. There are several connections in key areas between authentic leadership and these leadership principles from 1 Peter. Authentic leaders are those who have certain qualities like knowing who they are and what they believe in and are consistent in values, ethics, and actions as well as are known for their integrity (Gardner & Avolio, 2005). This self-identity is ontological having to do with the inner person and finds similarities with the ontological principle in 1 Peter of leaders living in a new self-identity and helping others with this process. The concept of authentic leadership assumes that a strong sense of self-identity is essential for this type of leadership (Klenke, 2007). In addition, the changed perspective of the person leads to leading with good ethics and integrity as found in the principles of Peter. Authentic leadership is defined in large part by evidence of morality in the leadership process which drives virtuous leadership (Hannah et al., 2005). Both concepts of leadership concern the identity of the person in that they are ontological in nature and they lead to virtuous leadership through ethics and morality.

Relationships in authentic leadership are characterized by openness, guidance toward worthy objectives, and an emphasis on follower development and produce positive follower development and outcomes (Mitchie & Gooty, 2005). One of the principles from Peter is the use of authority in caring for and guiding followers. In addition, leaders not only live in purpose themselves but help followers develop in purpose and destiny as well. This guidance and careful follower development is an issue of leadership in both of these aspects of leadership from Peter and from authentic leadership. The principles in Peter include a further component of finding and living in destiny and purpose, but this could be found as well in the self-identity concept of authentic leadership. Authentic leadership development is a process that fosters greater self-awareness in the person (Gardner & Avolio, 2005). This self-awareness and sense of purpose can be closely related in the process of working through self-issues as seen in both sets of concepts. Additionally, authentic leadership is not just concerned with leadership it is also concerned with the development process of becoming a leader. These principles from Peter share a similar concern in the development of leaders as a process and how that process occurs.

The spiritual identity system in authentic leadership is built in part on self-sacrifice, in addition, they consider sacrifice an integral component of leadership (Klenke, 2007). In 1 Peter, suffering is considered a key component to transformation, a new identity, joy, and strength as well as the development of integrity and trust. These are key components in 1 Peter of leadership principles. Here suffering is reconfigured from a result of judgment and evil to a process of testing in preparation for developing ontological issues in the person that are an integral part of leadership. The leader is transformed ontologically and leads from this reality. Authentic leaders influence followers by positively constructing reality for themselves and followers (Gardner & Avolio, 2005). The leaders, according to Peter's principles, are constructing a new reality for themselves and their followers. Both constructs include similarities that are important to ontology, the issue of being or the inner person, and the issue of reality and its discovery. The premise of Klenke's (2007) model of authentic leadership is that spirituality and spiritual identity are at the core of this type of leadership. Principles from Peter for leadership would find agreement with this need for spirituality and spiritual identity. Peter's call for suffering and following the Lord in his way of leadership call for spirituality in connection with God and in identifying with the Lord in following His example of leadership.

Nevertheless, this connection in spirituality begins to show the difference between the two systems as well. Authentic leadership calls for spirituality and spiritual identity with a focus on self and self-disclosure whereas 1 Peter calls for a spiritual identity that is in imitation of the Lord or to learn life and leadership from a mimesis of the Lord. This spiritual identity has ramifications for self and a new identity as well as a new reality, but it calls for a radical and personal connection to the Lord that result in a particular kind of leadership in the picture of Christ as shepherd and overseer. The focus is not on the self but on the Lord. Transparency is not the goal here but a reflection of the Lord and His leadership. The mimetic aspect of the leadership in Peter sets it apart from the model of authentic leadership with a different kind of focus moving from self to the Lord Himself. The center of authentic leadership is self. This self is refined, transparent, careful, and has a new identity as a person of trust and integrity. But this is not the same as endorsed by Peter. The leader in 1 Peter is one who has been changed, but to bring glory to God with a focus on eternal issues and glory to God, not simply being effective in accomplishing a task. Is good leadership simply being the most effective in influence and task accomplishment? First Peter challenges an affirmation of this question. The principles in Peter would have the leader be a shepherd and a steward, not just one who guides but one uses their gifts properly in leadership and power paradoxically. Again, this is in imitation of the Lord, in using power not for domination but as examples even in weakness.

Principles from Peter continue by endorsing the deep need for humility and vision for the future that affects the present. Though both of these may be seen in other issues in authentic leadership, these are not the issues of authentic leadership. Nevertheless, they are significant issues in the principles for leadership drawn from 1 Peter. Humility here is to be toward others, in connection to God, and is to be self-induced not just as a result of external incidents. The ontological changes in Peter include ethics and integrity like authentic leadership but expand beyond this perspective to deep personal humility and perseverance or fierce resolve similar to the findings by J. Collins (2001) in level 5 leadership or great leaders. Peter is instructing these leaders for the bigger picture: the vision of the future that affects the present as well as for greatness.

Authentic leadership and principles of leadership from the text of 1 Peter have many similarities. These areas of similarity include profound issues such as the ontology of leadership and the need for sacrifice or suffering, as well as the need for unique leadership development. They even share an aspect of spirituality and spiritual identity. However, on examination of the deeper issues it is found that there are some significant and important differences. These differences include a mimesis of the Lord in leadership as well as models of leadership in the images of shepherd and steward. The focus in authentic leadership for bearings and strength is the authentic self, whereas in principles for leadership in 1 Peter, bearings and strength are found in imitation of Christ as the Chief Shepherd and leader. The further differences are found in the focus on the ontological issues of humility and perseverance as found in Peter and the need for a clear vision of the future affecting the present. It is not a difference so much in behavior but a difference in motivation and focus which will result in a different kind of leadership. The one, authentic leadership, will lead to effective influence while the other to effective impact that is present and future.

Though Peter lived in the shade of towering figures like Paul ...he nevertheless cast his own distinctive theological shadow... No one is likely to be more directly indebted to the teaching and impact of Christ Himself than Peter.
  Ben Witherington III

CHAPTER 17

PETER IN THE CONTEXT OF PAUL

A Pauline model for Biblical leadership gaining attention in the contemporary context is Kenotic leadership. Kenotic leadership is a contemporary theory of leadership developed from the teachings of Paul in Philippians 2:5-11 in the New Testament. This model of leadership has six major components as found in this pericope of Christian Scripture. These components are (a) Christological mimesis, (b) kenosis or self-emptying, (c) servant posturing, (d) humane orientation, (e) active humility, and (f) missional obedience (Bekker, 2009). It is significant that principles from 1 Peter for leadership and kenotic leadership are both drawn from the writings of the New Testament of the Christian Scriptures though by different human authors. Nevertheless, the question remains as to the similarity and differences in these concepts drawn from a similar source but by different authors of antiquity.

The first issue of kenotic leadership is mimesis or the imitation of Christ as found in Philippians 2:5-11. Paul in this text was giving instruction on Christian living and presenting Christ as the ultimate model (Hawthorne, 1983). He held up the example of Christ who gave up the status and privilege of heaven (Grudem, 1994). This was a call to imitate Jesus in this text which was also a call to imitate God using a *cursus pudorum* or way of ignominy and humiliation rather than using a *cursus honorum* or way of honor (Bekker, 2007b). In leadership principles in 1 Peter, this call to the imitation of God and of Christ is a major component. In 1 Peter, one is called to an imitation of Christ in suffering and in leadership, even rejecting the cultural way of honor instead adopting a life that will bring glory to God and grace for the individual. This focus in Peter is not upon the glory of Rome but upon the glory of God and in this process the individual is to live in suffering for Christ, providing a different way of honor in the midst of a shame and honor society in contradistinction to the norms of the cultural. This way of imitation of Christ contains issues of humiliation or suffering and seeking honor with God instead of honor with the society or culture in which one lives.

The second issue in kenotic leadership is that of kenosis. Kenosis is the concept of the self-emptying of one's will and becoming entirely receptive and responsible to God's perfect will and Jesus Christ is the example of this process (Danley, 2009). The word *kenosis* is translated in Philippians 2:7 as "made Himself nothing" and comes from the word meaning "to empty" (Hardgrove, 2008). When Christ emptied himself, He effaced all thought of Himself and poured himself out to enrich others (Hawthorne, 1983). This provides an example and an alternate form of Christian leadership of the radical giving up of status and privilege in leadership in union with Christ leading to personal transformation of both leaders and followers (Bekker, 2006). The process of becoming receptive and responsible to the will of God is found in the context of the principles of leadership in 1 Peter. Leaders in Peter are exhorted to live in the purpose of God for themselves and to help followers live in the purpose of God as well. In 1 Peter, leadership is based upon transformed relationships and transformation of the person in helping others by focusing on the actualization of God's purpose in the transformation of the person. In addition, the steward leader in 1 Peter learns to use power paradoxically not in domination like God did in revealing his power through weakness on the cross. At the center of the principles for leadership found in 1 Peter is the concept of transformation of the individual through a proper response to suffering. This proper response in suffering transforms the person developing purity, strength, joy, and a new identity. Then leaders help followers through this same transformation process. However, this internal process in the leader is an ontological change as well in emptying self and the imitation of Christ. In Peter, a leader is changing ontologically in becoming a different person through transformation in the inner person and leading through a changed perspective and reality which then affects their behavior. This is the same process as seen in kenotic leadership of emptying self, personal transformation, and leading in ways that are not based upon status and privilege. Kenosis in leadership and principles as found in 1 Peter contain some profound and significant similarities in this particular area.

The third step in kenotic leadership is taking the form of a servant. This does not speak of mere service but of the radical quest to take the form of a slave (Bekker, 2006). Christ, in this context, understood His position to mean giving instead of getting (O'Brien, 1991). This kenotic concept of becoming a servant is ontological, not just behavioral. In principles of leadership found in 1 Peter, there is an ontological change for the leader. This change includes a new identity and a new reality that affects the ethics, values, and behavior of the leader. In addition, the leader is to imitate Christ in His suffering and in His model as a servant and to become a steward leader. A steward or *oikonomos* was a domestic servant, a reliable slave with authority delegated by the householder or owner and Paul in another place uses this word to describe himself, Apollos, and Peter as servants of Christ (Elliot, 2000). However, the more prominent exhortation is to follow Christ as the Chief Shepherd. In this description of the leaders as shepherds, they are exhorted to lead not as masters but as examples and not for what they can gain instead for what they can give and to do it according to the will of God. Both kenotic leadership and principles from 1 Peter includes an exhortation to ontological change having to do with becoming a servant and leading through giving to others rather than trying to receive from them.

The fourth step in the kenotic model of leadership comes from the fact that Christ was found in the form of a man. This is a relinquishment of self for the sake of others; it is a shared recognition of shared humanity with others (Reid, 2009). This shared humanity proposes a praxis of charity, identification with one being served, and authentic love in the exercise of leadership (Bekker, 2007b). This identification with the followers and practice of charity is seen in 1 Peter in the leader not only working through the process of suffering but in helping others work through the process of suffering to transformation, and leadership in Peter is based on transformed relationships. In other words, there is a relational connection between leader and follower in the leader partnering with the follower for transformation in ontological as well as relational aspects. Kenosis involves suffering as well (Reid, 2009). So, there are several connections here between kenotic leadership and principles from 1 Peter for the leadership process. In addition, leaders in 1 Peter are not only to live in purpose and their calling they are to help others live out their life fulfilling their purpose as well. Kenotic leadership involves the leader having a shared identity with followers expressed in charity and principles from 1 Peter involves the practical application of this shared identity by the leaders helping the follower develop purpose and transform through suffering. It is significant as well that both concepts from kenotic and Peter involve suffering.

The fifth step in kenotic leadership is that of humility imitating Christ in His humility. In this text in Philippians 2:8, the verb is reflexive meaning to "humble oneself"; it was a deliberate act of self-humiliation and this action was free and voluntary (O'Brien, 1991). This self-humbling as a voluntary act is found again in 1 Peter in the exhortation to leaders to humble themselves and to clothe themselves with humility. This call to humility includes the voluntary rejection of symbols, and systems of power, prestige, and privilege. (Bekker, 2006). In 1 Peter the leadership principles include a rejection of the cultural models of prestige and honor while using power paradoxically, in the way of suffering or, as Luther called it (Althaus, 1966), the way of the cross. Humility was central to the Christian ethic in this era and Peter told the leaders they were to model this virtue in following their Chief Shepherd (Witherington, 2007). Profound humility that is entered and developed freely is an important aspect of both kenotic leaders and leadership principles as found in 1 Peter.

In the final step in kenotic leadership, the obedience of Christ in death becomes the model for leaders to obey the model of the Lord in developing humane leadership that is humble and not focused on upward mobility. The practical application is clear that obedience to this alternative view of leadership would bring dishonor to the readers of these texts but it would bring honor in Christ and ultimate reality; this is a call to abandon social honor and to follow the new way of leadership as set forth by Christ (Bekker, 2007b). It has already been seen that principles of leadership from 1 Peter include a countercultural way of leading. However, it also includes leading according to the will of God and for the glory that is both present and future. This participation in the glory is a new reality both present and future. This new reality includes a reconfiguration of suffering, holiness, and leadership. These leaders are to lead with obedience in mind in imitating the Lord in shepherding the flock of God. Obedience is important here in this leadership since the leaders will receive a crown of glory from the Chief Shepherd for this way of leadership. In addition, the leadership in 1 Peter includes a perseverance or fierce resolve in resisting the enemy and leading others. This perseverance is a long-term obedience in following the Lord and leading others. Kenotic leadership and principles for leadership in 1 Peter both include obedience to the Lord in leading in a way that is countercultural but is imperative for effective leading in imitation of God rather than social norms.

Power (1998) added that in kenosis that Jesus brings a role of radical reversal of authority and power to those called to leadership, one that undermines relationships of domination and control that have characterized human society. This type of kenotic leadership is not only countercultural, it specifically critiques normal uses of authority and power. Principles for leadership from 1 Peter offer this same critique in that authority is to be used in guiding and caring for the followers not as a reward and punishment. In addition, the leaders in Peter are specifically told not to lord or take dominion over followers. This role reversal, though counterintuitive, is an important part of the leadership concepts in both areas.

This imitation of Christ is the reformation of the human nature through conformity to Christ (Herdt, 2008). A school of thought has developed around the idea that the most important human motive is that of mimesis which is not just to imitate others it is also to imitate their desires which facilitate learning and empathy in individuals (Webb, 2009). This reforming the human nature of the inner person is training that affects the person ontologically. It is possible for people to change in their inner being and in their sense of reality, both ontological issues. Kenotic leadership implies the training process in the application of this type of leadership. The Petrine concepts of leadership also imply mimesis and ontological change in the process of becoming leaders. The Petrine model adds the concept of proper response to suffering in this process but as we have seen kenosis also involves suffering in its model. Both areas of leadership kenotic and Petrine also include humility as part of the process of becoming leaders. There are implications for Petrine leadership development in inclusion of theological and historical issues but these same issues come to the fore in the kenotic model since it is also an issue of leadership based in Scripture and the history of the church.

There is one issue that leadership in 1 Peter presented as a principle that is not explicit in the kenotic model. This principle is that of a proper vision of the future for a proper perspective of the present. In discussing the future judgment, Peter was concerned that the people saw clearly what was to come, particularly leaders—since judgment would start with them—so they would know how to live, suffer, and lead in the present. Vision is seen in other models to be an important aspect of leadership (Bass, 1990, Yukl, 2002). Breisach (2007) said people live in the past, present, and future simultaneously. Therefore, it is important to see the future to lead in the present. It is seen in the Petrine model as an important component as well. This is the one area that Peter added to the kenotic thinking about leadership.

Kenotic leadership and principles of leadership as found in 1 Peter are very similar ways of thinking about and doing leadership. They address similar issues and in ways that are not only similar but congruently counterintuitive and countercultural. To strengthen this thought is the fact that they are both drawn from the New Testament though from different pericopes and by different human authors. Nevertheless, there is great conformity among the two systems of thinking. The one area of difference is that of vision for the future which is promoted in 1 Peter but not in the kenotic model. Nevertheless, the question is whether the concept of vision is implicit in one of the issues of the kenotic model. It is possible that though both models are from Christian Scripture that the Petrine principles simply expand the model given in the Philippians correspondence. Either way, the overwhelming evidence is for these concepts of leadership to be considered similar if not rooted in the same model. It is possible that Paul and Peter were working from a model of leadership that they understood, endorsed, and promoted with slight variations for the purpose of developing effective leadership in the church.

Both saw Jesus Christ as the model for life and for leadership who is to be imitated on some very profound level that affects the ontology of the person. This ontological change in the person changes the inner person as well as the behavior of the leader. In addition, both concepts for leadership emphasize humility and a new use of power and authority that is counter to human cultures and thinking. These similarities in leadership principles are both profound and consistent, showing these concepts to be helpful in strengthening a model of leadership from the Christian Scriptures.

We recognize that Peter transfers his legacy and the legacy of Christ in the message to the elders and followers of God's church. In this letter from Peter, we see a model for servant leadership and recognize the importance of mentoring our own leaders to develop their character.
   Kevin Leahy

CHAPTER 18

PETER IN THE CONTEXT OF THE CHURCH

The text of 1 Peter was written to and in the context of the church, therefore these principles of leadership are significant for leadership in the contemporary church as the descendants of these church leaders in 1 Peter. These ten principles find their root in the theology of the New Testament and their application initially in the context of the community of believers living as aliens and strangers in the world and its systems. Therefore, the implications and applications of these principles can be directly applied to ecclesial leadership in its contemporary context. Further, it is relevant to the church in that the church has followed a business model for leadership when another model more significant for the church is available. The pressure to succeed in bringing more people into the church has led to the adoption of a business style approach with a business model of leadership in the church (McGrath, 2002). However, to re-establish God's design for the church, it is crucial to understand biblical leadership to discover how to lay a biblical foundation to rebuild church leadership (Damazio, 1988). Leadership in the church follows the business model in many ways and this is understandable as the church exists in the same culture as the businesses around them. However, in many ways, the church follows the culture around them, but this was the precise issue that Peter was addressing in 1 Peter. He was challenging the believers to live and lead in such a way that was countercultural and even challenging to the systems that were prominent at the time. It is possible that this call to challenge cultural bound leadership with timeless principles of leadership was not just a 1st-century issue but it is also a 21st-century issue. In many ways, the church follows the culture. However, the church needs to lead and critique culture, not simply follow it. This area of leadership is one area where the church has been given principles and instruction that are important and countercultural. It is possible that the church could critique and challenge human culture in this area of leadership. This challenge could come in developing principles and concepts for leadership in the church based upon biblical principles in that the church could lead the world of business in this area rather than follow. There is a call here for a truly biblical leadership in building church leadership but in also leading the culture instead of following in developing effective ways of leading others.

Principle 1 in principles of leadership from 1 Peter is about transformation through suffering. Suffering is part of the process of preparation for leadership and learning to respond properly to it. In this process, transformation takes place in the leader developing the core of character, a new identity, strength, and joy. In this process, these individuals also develop integrity and the ability to develop trust in followers. Then the leaders who have walked through this suffering transformation help the followers through this same process. Suffering is recontextualized in a way that is paradoxical. Even though it appears to be the result of evil, it is really for development. Potential leaders in the church need to learn to respond well to the suffering in their life, not to pursue it simply to respond in the midst of it. Leadership in the church needs to be based on the transformation of the life of the leader, whose life is characterized by integrity, trustworthiness, and a new identity of character, strength, and joy.

Principle 2 is closely related to the first in the need for ontological change or change in one's being and perspective of reality. This transformation in the inner person of the leader is ontological; it is not simply a change of behavior. However, ontological change in the inner person produces changed behavior and a changed perspective concerning reality. In the church, there needs to be a new emphasis here on the person or the inner person of the leader focusing on character development and developing a new sense of identity in connection to the new reality of the present and future glory. When one embraces and understands suffering that has been recontextualized it becomes a source of character. In the church, leadership needs to be based in character and values not simply established on a behavior model. Leadership is ontological in that it proceeds from the person and their perception of reality. The leader leads from a new sense of identity and reality in helping others in this new identity and reality. Leadership is about people and transformation that is ontological before it is about behavior and the world's concept of success. This leadership is countercultural in that it is not the normal way of implied leadership.

Principle 3 in leadership that is Petrine is that it is mimetic it involves an imitation of God and Christ. This particularly separates this leadership from other business models. Christ is the shepherd that cares for the followers, the overseer who guides the followers, and the suffering servant who sets the example for followers. There are specific ways that Christ is to be imitated as the shepherd in leading by example or as a role model, leading by giving not trying to get something, and with the proper attitude not promoting self. Each of these ways are counterintuitive but are to be accomplished in imitating Christ in His leadership. Significantly, this leadership for the church is different than domineering leadership and leadership for gain or promotion. While providing a role model to follow is considered as a leadership quality (Kouzes & Posner, 2007), this mimesis of the Lord provides specific concrete issues or ways that are to be modeled. Leadership in the church needs to imitate the model of the Lord in leading instead of the model of the business leader. This is not to critique the business model as wrong, simply to add insights that are eternal for effective leadership.

Principle 4 is the proper use of authority in Petrine leadership. Authority involves the rights, duties, and powers associated with a particular position and it can be used in ways that are either careful of domineering. The Petrine model of the use of authority endorses using authority in caring for and guiding the followers rather than in dominance. Leaders in the church are to use and learn to use authority carefully not simply using it for task accomplishment but using it to guide followers in them finding and fulfilling their purpose as well as providing care for the followers. This is authority with people and transformation in mind rather than authority to reinforce position or will.

Steward leadership is Principle 5 in the Petrine leadership principles. This steward leader is a servant leader who serves by overseeing the house; he or she leads as a servant. This servant leader uses the gifts given to them wisely in the effective leadership of the community not to gain honor or status. This divesting of prestige and power inherent in the leadership transaction allows the leader and follower to have a new relationship based in equality and service (Bekker, 2007b). This is servant leadership that develops partnerships and transformed relationships in the community for effective leadership. This steward leader also uses power paradoxically. This use of power is to show the glory of God and reveal His character rather than as a way to human desire. This leadership is centered on God and His purpose and will rather than the desire and glory of humans. Leadership in the church is to use power paradoxically like God does in helping people to change and transform in the midst of suffering and weakness not in oppressing the weak.

In the principles for leadership found in 1 Peter, the sixth principle is having a vision of the future. Peter wanted the leaders to see the present in light of the future since this would give a true perspective of the present and how one was to live in the present. Vision is an important aspect of leadership even in the business models (Canton, 2007; Kouzes & Posner, 2007; Yukl, 2002). Vision helps not only see but create the future (Canton, 2007). Vision is an important aspect for leadership in the church in two ways. One way is to see the reward ahead and live life courageously in light of that coming reward. The other way that vision is important is to see God's design for the future and to begin to lead in that direction; the leader is to help others in finding and fulfilling the purpose of God which is present and future oriented. Leadership in the church needs to be visionary leadership.

The seventh principle is that of perseverance or fierce resolve. This is also recognized in business models (J. Collins, 2001) as an important ingredient for effective leadership. The proper response to suffering is perseverance and faith and the key is fierce resolve to pass through the trouble. This perseverance helps the leader walk through difficult situations and difficult times or even in dealing with difficult people. The ability to do this in the leader provides the ability of the leader in helping others through suffering, trouble, and difficulty. Leaders in the church are those who persevere and are faithful even in difficulties.

The eighth principle is that a leader in the church needs to live in the purpose of God, in their particular call and destiny as well as help others find their purpose and destiny. Destiny is important to individuals and helping other find it is an important aspect of leaders helping, encouraging, and directing followers. Finding this call is important because it is the foundation of one of the deepest sources of self-discovery and growth in life and it gives inspiration and dynamism to individuals (Guinness, 2003). The leader encourages people and helps give momentum to followers in this way, producing effective direction and life for the community. This is an ontological issue as well in helping others to develop in their inner person and as growth and momentum happens in the individual it happens as well in the church.

Principle 9 in Petrine leadership is the key component of humility. This is not self-degradation in any way. Humility in its purest form is the greatest source of personal power and is the key to true leadership according to Benedict of Nursia who established a long standing effective method of leadership (Galbraith & Galbraith, 2004). Peter told the leaders to model the virtue of humility in following Christ as the Chief Shepherd in 1 Peter (Witherington, 2007). Humility in leadership, like many of the other principles here, is counterculturalal and it is also counterintuitive. This way of leadership in humility not only is in imitation of Christ, it also as a model for others to follow in humility. In this way, humility is an important characteristic to model for the development of humility in all the individuals in the community. There are a few business models that endorse humility as a main ingredient of leadership in spite of its countercultural nature. One of these is Level 5 leadership as developed by J. Collins (2001). In this way of humility, the leader does not promote self but instead promotes participation in overcoming the deleterious effects of pride and self-focused leadership. One of the hallmarks of leadership in the church needs to be this quality of humility. Humility is ontological but it affects behavior on several levels from motive to actions.

Principle 10 in Petrine leadership concerns leadership development. Leadership development is a concern for all types of organizations since all organizations need leadership.

However, leadership in the church could look different than other models for leadership development. Day (2000) discussed the strengths and weaknesses of different models of development including 360-degree feedback, mentoring, coaching, and instruction. Nevertheless, these models do not get to the core of the issue of what is to be developed. Many models endeavor to develop behaviors (Northouse, 2004; Yukl, 2002). However, the model presented in the text of 1 Peter endorses leadership development as a process of learning to respond properly to suffering. In this setting, one is to imitate Christ who suffered by responding with perseverance and a proper focus producing new strength and a new perspective of reality. The ancient process of education was that of imitation as is found in the concepts of 1 Peter. This process transforms the person ontologically. The point is ontological transformation since leadership in this text is an ontological issue. In addition, training for humility is important in learning the proper perspective in living as well as in leading others. Then leadership is set in the context of theology and antiquity showing the need for understanding in these areas of theology and history. Leadership development in the Petrine way of leading needs development in theology as well as history to set the context and then training in transformation through suffering to become the leader ontologically and in humility. This development for leaders is countercultural but it is the necessary way of development that is based in the theological underpinnings of this text and to bring the ontological changes necessary for this type of leadership.

The ramifications for church leadership from the principles of leadership of 1 Peter are significant. This is a way of leadership and leadership development that is not only countercultural, but it is also sensitive to eternal issues of theology that are important to the church. This leadership in Peter is specifically designed for leading the church in antiquity and in contemporary settings as well. The implications are that if the church could begin to find the biblical foundation for leadership it could bring new ground for the church in effectiveness and in leading the culture rather than following it.

The study of leadership is concerned with the understanding of reality...In this adventure leadership and spirituality should not be enemies, but rather close friends.
Corne' Bekker

CHAPTER 19

PETER IN THE CONTEXT OF CONTEMPORARY BUSINESS

Since these concepts for leadership are rooted in theology and applied in the context of the church, can they have any relevance in the organizational world? Organizations face many of the same issues as the church. The model for the church should provide a model for the organizational world to follow as well. The church has the advantage of documents from antiquity that speak to the issues, but this does not prevent the organizational world from benefitting from these principles of leadership. The theological base provides a strong foundation and a broad perspective but these principles can still be set in an organizational context for effective leadership. In addition, there is at least one other model that is drawn from Scripture and history that has been applied to the organizational world, that of Galbraith and Galbraith (2004). They take the teaching of Benedict of Nursia, which are heavily founded in Scriptures both Old and New Testaments, and discover concepts of leadership that are then applied directly to organizational contexts. This process of applying biblical truth to organizational contexts has precedent and the Scriptures by design were intended to impact the human culture and this is one important way for this impact.

Principle 1 in 1 Peter is transformation through suffering, and it includes issues like integrity and trust as well as good character and ethics. These attributes are important issues for organizational leadership. Most scholars consider integrity as a requirement for ethical leadership even in studies that cross cultures (Yukl, 2002). Ethics needs to be at the heart of leadership with issues such as honesty, integrity, and trustworthiness (Ciulla, 2004). Guinness (2000) challenged leaders to return to an emphasis on character rather than externals.

Clearly, organizational leadership needs these issues developed in leaders, however, can the process of transformation through suffering be useful in the organizational context?

It is evident that all people suffer whether believers or not. Nevertheless, the question remains as to whether these sufferings can be reconfigured for transformation of the person. It is the understanding of the suffering and persevering through it that brings transformation through a reconfiguration of the concept of suffering. Organizational leaders go through trouble and disasters. In fact, one of the key concepts for leaders in Kouzes and Posner's (2007) model for leadership is to challenge the process and in transformational leadership (Yukl, 2002) it is intellectual stimulation which both include an awareness of problems and a view of problems from a new perspective. Therefore, in many ways, these issues of suffering, transformation, good character, and integrity are called for in organizational leadership in diverse models. A reconfiguration of suffering for transformation in the process of developing a new perspective as well as integrity, trustworthiness, and good ethics is applicable and important to organizational leadership contexts. This first principle in 1 Peter could be part of the development process for leaders in an organizational context.

Principle 2 in 1 Peter for leadership is closely related to the first that of ontological change in the inner person and the change in the perception of reality. This ontological change results in a new identity and a changed perspective through which one leads. Can organizational leaders embrace ontological not just behavioral change? In authentic leadership, the clarity of one's possible authentic self, coupled with the drive to attain this possible self, can provide strong motivation for self-development toward authenticity and we know developmentally that the complexity and strength of one's self-beliefs can be advanced in making sense of stimuli and acquire new knowledge (Gardner et al., 2005). This authentic leadership as a contemporary model for organizational leadership not only allows for the possibility for internal change but calls for this change in the development of leadership. In addition, authentic leadership calls for a new perspective on reality as well. Leaders energize followers by positively constructing reality for themselves first and then for their followers (Avolio et al., 2004). Constructing reality and internal change are important ingredients for the leadership principles in 1 Peter and can be applied to organizational leadership contexts.

Principle 3 in leadership principles from 1 Peter is that leadership is mimetic in imitation of God and Christ in their leadership. This call to mimesis is leadership in the images or models of shepherd, overseer, and servant. The practical issues that come from these images are: (a) leading by example or role model, (b) leading by giving rather than in trying to gain something, and (c) leading not with force but in serving. Can this imitation occur in organizational contexts? The essence of ancient education was following good models or imitating other people (Witherington, 2007). Kouzes and Posner (2007) declared that an important component for contemporary effective leadership is to provide a role model. The implications are that individuals can learn and change through following role models. In modern leadership development models, Day (2000) promoted the idea of mentoring. According to Clinton (1988), one of the functions of a mentor is to provide a model for the student to follow. Imitation is an important concept for leadership development in contemporary settings. This is imitation in specific issues. One is leading by example, however, if the leader is to follow the example of Christ then it is possible for the follower to follow the example of the leader particularly in light of the instructions to organizational leaders from Kouzes and Posner (2007) and Day (2000). A leader can imitate someone as a role model in preparation to provide a role model for followers. When it comes to leading by giving to others and leading by serving, can these be applied in this contemporary setting as well? Servant leadership, a contemporary theory of organizational leadership, calls for the leaders to lead by serving (Patterson, 2003). Serving is the primary function of servant leadership not based on self-interest but based upon the interest of others (Farling, Stone, & Winston, 1999). Serving in light of the interest of others not for self-promotion is the main principle of servant leadership which is a contemporary theory for organizational leadership. Leading by mimesis, in imitation of Christ, who led by example, by giving, and serving, not forcefully, is a component of leadership from the principles of Peter that can be applied to organizational leadership.

Principle 4 of leadership principles from 1 Peter is the proper use of authority in caring for and guiding followers. This caring guidance is in contradistinction to using power for self-promotion or using it in domineering ways. This is an important issue in organizational leadership. Authority involves the rights of a particular position to exercise power and success and depends on the manner in which this power is exercised; effective leaders use power carefully not in arrogance or with manipulation (Yukl, 2002). Wise use of this power according to Petrine principles would be in caring for and guiding followers, which is in contradistinction to arrogance and manipulation. In addition, Kouzes and Posner (2007) showed that an important quality for effective leadership is encouraging the heart of their followers and an important aspect of this encouragement is showing care for followers. Proper use of authority in caring for and guiding followers is an important component for organizational leadership.

The fifth principle of Petrine principles of leadership is becoming a steward or servant leader who properly uses the gifts given to them and at the same time uses power paradoxically. Servant leadership has already been seen as an important concept for contemporary leadership. Servant leadership is about focus and the focus is on the followers and the leader's attitude and behavior are congruent with this follower focus; this theory is based in virtuous theory one of the oldest theories of Western philosophy (Patterson, 2003). This servant leader uses power paradoxically not as a source of will but of help to the followers. Leaders must learn to use power paradoxically since giving power away results in more power (Kouzes & Posner, 2007). The steward leader is an image of a servant with authority but who uses the power paradoxically not for establishing human will but in giving power to and encouraging followers. Senge (2006) described an important aspect of leadership in learning organizations is that of being a steward. This steward leadership is a component of the Petrine principles of leadership that can be effective in organizational leadership settings.

Principle 6 in leadership, according to 1 Peter, is vision in an ability to see the future for a proper perspective for the present. Vision is an important component of contemporary leadership models like servant leadership (Patterson, 2003) and transformational leadership (Bass, 1990; Yukl, 2002). It is also endorsed for effective leaders generally (Canton, 2007; Kouzes & Posner, 2007). Effective leaders see their vision as an important part of something larger than themselves as a part of the organization (Northouse, 2004). Visionary leadership as a principle of leadership from the principles of 1 Peter is also an integral part of organizational leadership.

Principle 7 in leadership principles from 1 Peter is perseverance or fierce resolve. This fierce resolve produces firmness in the leader and the ability to pass through times of trouble. Fierce resolve is one of the two important qualities for level 5 or great leaders according to J. Collins (2001). In describing virtues of leadership according to Benedict of Nursia, Galbraith and Galbraith (2004) described the rule of iron resolve as fortitude and inner strength. Part of the foundation of leadership is bulldog resolve that is strenuous and determined (Galbraith & Galbraith, 2004). This fierce resolve involves perseverance and inner strength according to Peter and contemporary leadership thinking. Leadership resolve is a component for organizational leadership.

Principle 8 for leadership from 1 Peter is that a leader needs to live in purpose or destiny and help others live in purpose and their calling as well. Guinness (2003) sayid that calling is for everyone everywhere and that this living in calling is the source of deep self-discovery and growth for the individual. Leaders help others learn new skills and develop existing talents as well as provide support for ongoing growth and change and turning the followers into leaders through understanding and having empathy for each of the followers (Kouzes & Posner, 2007). This focus on each follower to help them develop their gifts is a way of helping them in the process of self-discovery and calling. Strategic leadership relates to assessing where one is and then moving to the understanding of who one is and finally understanding where one should go (Hughes & Beatty, 2005). The effective leader discovers talents, personhood, and direction, which is one's calling and then helps followers to discover these same things. This is a relevant aspect of leadership for organizational leadership in the contemporary context.

Principle 9 for leadership from 1 Peter is the attribute of humility and its development. This humility is not self-degradation but as part of leadership it sets an example for others to follow in living in this state of humility. In 2001, J. Collins brought humility into the discussion of leadership calling it one of the two indispensible ingredients of great leadership. In addition, Galbraith and Galbraith (2004) declared that the pinnacle of leadership in the Benedictine system is the paradox between iron resolve and deep personal humility. Winston (2002) discussed humility as one of the seven principles for values-based leadership. In addition, Patterson (2003) put forth humility as an important ingredient to servant leadership. Humility is a personal orientation based on the willingness to see self accurately and a propensity to put oneself in perspective involving neither self-abasement nor overly positive self-regard (Morris, Brotheridge, & Urbanski, 2005). Humility is an integral aspect of leadership according 1 Peter and it has been found to be important in leadership effectiveness in both antiquity and in contemporary thinking and it is relevant in contemporary organizational leadership.

Principle 10 of leadership principles in 1 Peter concerns leadership development. This process of leadership development involves learning to respond properly to suffering for transformation that is ontological. This process also involves mimesis and the development of humility as well as the study of theology and history. Leadership development is an important issue for contemporary leadership as discussed by Day (2000), as it is found in many different forms. Can leadership development happen in the process of learning to respond to suffering? Suffering once it is reconfigured it begins to change the person. This change is the necessary ingredient for the development of leaders who lead ethically and by example. Suffering reconfigured has the purpose of purification. One of the issues of transformational leadership is the ability to view problems from a new perspective (Yukl, 2002). In addition, authentic leadership calls for a new perspective on reality both for the leader and for helping the follower. This new reality can come through this process of understanding suffering reconfigured in the development process. This development is through the process of imitation. Can imitation work in the contemporary context. Some of the concepts of development involve on the job training (Day, 2000). This type of training involves watching and then doing, which is the essence of imitation.

In addition, the Petrine development process includes training for humility. Can humility be developed? Like godly character and integrity it must be developed in the internal being of the person but this process can happen, in fact it must happen, for effective leadership. Good character is important to leadership as it provides the deepest source of bearings and strongest source of restraint (Guinness, 2000). Humility can be cultivated and nurtured by an ascending path of knowledge included with time and patience (Galbraith & Galbraith, 2004). Humility can be developed in a person through a process of learning.

Finally, history and theology are part of the Petrine development process. Guinness (2000) encouraged a search for the remedy to the crisis of leadership by looking back in history for wisdom and direction, and this look into history includes both the Hebrew and Christian Scriptures. The task of historians is to trace the ways in which people have reflected on the past and what these reflections have told them about human life, and one of the functions of history is that of teacher (Breisach, 2007). This function of teacher could include history as found in Scripture as well. Leadership development as a process of reconfiguring suffering, learning the way of humility, and gaining insight from history possibly even Scripture could be brought into the contemporary organizational context for the development of leaders who could then be transformed ontologically in preparation to lead by example.

Each of these ten principles from 1 Peter finds their application in contemporary leadership thinking and models. These principles relate to several diverse models of leadership and they come together in this concept for leadership. These principles for leadership from 1 Peter for organizational leadership can be seen in the following list: (a) reconfiguration of suffering for transformation for integrity, trustworthiness, ethics, (b) ontological change with a new identity and new sense of reality, (c) mimetic in imitation of Christ, lead by example, giving, serving, (d) proper use of authority in encouraging followers, (e) steward leader or servant leader with a follower focus using power paradoxically, (f) vision to see the future for proper perspective for the present, (g) fierce resolve to lead with fortitude and inner strength, (h) live in calling and purpose and empower others by helping them walk in their purpose, (i) humility – to see self accurately, and (j) leadership development by reconfiguring suffering, developing humility, studying history. These ten principles work together in a system of leadership for the church in 1 Peter in antiquity; they can be formed together for the contemporary church and for organizational leadership in the contemporary context. In Peter these concepts are deeply connected with one's connection to God and spirituality. However, in the organizational setting these principles can be used for effective leadership based on the text of 1 Peter.

It is presumptuous to act as if leadership philosophy was born in the twentieth century...Leadership theory is firmly grounded in the archives of history.
  Craig Galbraith and Oliver Galbraith III

CHAPTER 20

CONCLUSION – ANCIENT WISDOM IN CONTEXT

Ten principles were found in this study from an exegetical socio-rhetorical study of the text of 1 Peter. These principles were then applied for ecclesial leadership and organizational leadership. These ten principles could be applied in either setting. However, it is important for the church to begin to examine, discuss, and adopt biblical principles of leadership instead of following the ways of the culture in leadership. Peter was addressing this issue in 1 Peter in giving another way of leadership in the imitation of Christ. The call here is for the church to examine the root of current leadership models and definitions of effectiveness. The imitation of the business models has brought some good results but is this the conclusion of the matter? Is there more for the church in leadership as found in these texts? It is incumbent on the church to search this out and find firm foundations for leadership. The church should be able to lead in leadership concepts and principles rather than follow the culture. Though there are some similarities to different contemporary leadership models, these principles couple the issues of vision, with issues of character, and ontological change. These concepts held together in these principles from Peter provide a unique approach to leadership. This approach is valuable for both the church and modern organizations. These principles provide for the external as well as internal issues including issues of calling and leadership development. Together these principles provide a robust conceptual framework for leadership dealing with internal character issues as well as external issues of the proper use of power and authority.

It is significant that the examination of Scripture through socio-rhetorical analysis in this pericope has led to a few principles of leadership that could have an impact on leadership in the church and organizations. This area should be further developed in the broader context of all of Hebrew and Christian Scriptures. The way to perceive the present properly is to see the future but possibly the way into the future for leadership involves a look into the past. This is not a call for a few more studies in exegetical fashion but a call for a systematic development of exegetical study specifically on leadership in the whole of Hebrew and Christian Scriptures. This would have to be done one piece at a time but it should be a directed effort that is organized around the goal of looking at the full context of Scripture deeply for insights that could then be compared and applied to church and organizational leadership.

When compared to authentic leadership, these principles of leadership were found to be different than this contemporary model of leadership. However, there are some profound and important similarities. These similarities include spirituality as part of the foundation for leadership. In addition, authentic leadership contains issues of ontological change, including a new identity and a new perspective in reality. These are some important concepts for the leadership principles as found in 1 Peter not found in many other models of leadership. Though authentic leadership has a spiritual core and deals with issues of ontology the focus is developing an authentic self, whereas in Petrine leadership the focus is on the imitation of Christ and on transformation to be able to help others in the transformation process.

Kenotic leadership and principles of leadership found in 1 Peter have some profound and important connections and similarities. They are both drawn from the Christian Scriptures. They both focus on the imitation of Christ in His life and leadership. They both have a focus on becoming a servant and giving of self in humility. They both endorse a way of development that is in imitation of the example of Christ not just in behavior but also in attitude. These two concepts of leadership even share a call to radical reversal in the use of power and the normal way of honor in the human way of thinking. There is one area that principles from Peter expand beyond kenotic leadership. It is the area of vision. Many contemporary theories of leadership speak of vision and its development and power but the kenotic model does not. This is not a difference as much as thoughtful proposition of expansion for kenotic leadership. Nevertheless, the similarities and connections here are too broad and profound to be dismissed. This promotes the idea of more exegetical work to be able to develop more nuanced and profound theories of leadership from the context of Scripture.

These ten principles from Peter have potential impact for both church and organizational leadership. An area of profound impact could be the concept of leadership development through the process of reconfiguring suffering for transformation, putting a new focus on the process of humility development, and a deep study of theology and history in the context of leadership development. This type of leadership drawn from exegetical analysis of the Scriptures could have a profound effect on the church in helping the church develop more profound ways of leadership for the health of the church. In this process, this would set a model in the church for organizational leaders to follow. The church needs to become the leader in leadership not the distant follower of culture that changes with the winds of culture. Can the church be relevant and timeless in leadership? Peter thought they could. This would include the contemporary church as well.

These ten principles provide a roadmap for leadership development and the way of leadership that is ontological, mimetic, visionary, serving, paradoxically powerful, filled with humility, purpose, and fierce resolve. This combination in imitation of the Lord can provide profound help for leaders in many different contexts whether inside or outside of the church and help to provide a way ahead for leadership, leadership development, and leadership studies.

References

Althaus, P. (1966). *The theology of Martin Luther.* Minneapolis, MN: Fortress Press.

Anderson, L. (1997). *They smell like sheep: Spiritual leadership for the 21st century.* West Monroe, LA: Howard Books.

Avolio, B. J., Gardner, W. L., Walumbwa, W. O., & May, D. (2004). Unlocking the mask: A look at the process by which authentic leaders impact follower attitudes and behaviors. *Leadership Quarterly, 15*(6), 801-823.

Ayers, M. (2006). Towards a theology of leadership. *Journal of Biblical Perspectives in Leadership, 1*(1), 3-27.

Bass, B. M. (1990). *Bass & Stogdill's handbook of leadership: Theory, research, and managerial applications.* New York, NY: The Free Press.

Beardslee, W. A. (1994). What is it about? Reference in New Testament literary criticism. In E. McKnight & E. Malbon (Eds.), *The new literary criticism and the New Testament* (pp. 367-386). Valley Forge, PA: Trinity Press.

Bekker, C. J. (2005). *Kenotic mysticism and servant leadership in the letters of Clare of Assisi to Agnes of Prague.* Paper presented at Servant Leadership Research Roundtable, Virginia Beach, VA.

Bekker, C. J. (2006). *The Philippians hymn (2:5-11) as an early mimetic Christological model of Christian leadership in Roman Philippi.*

Paper presented at Servant Leadership Research Roundtable, Virginia Beach, VA.

Bekker, C. J. (2007a). *Dreaming with open eyes: Reflections on leadership and spirituality.* Retrieved from http://www.regent.edu/acad/global/publications/working/DreamingwithOpenEyes-ReflectionsonLeadershipandSpirituality-Bekker2007.pdf

Bekker. C. J. (2007b). *Sharing the incarnation: Towards a model of mimetic Christological leadership.* Paper presented at the Biblical Perspectives Research Roundtable, Virginia Beach, VA.

Bekker, C. J. (2008). The turn to spirituality and downshifting. In F. Gandolfi & C. Cherrier (Eds.), *Downshifting: A theoretical and practical approach to living a simple life* (pp. 102-121). Hyderabad: ICFAI Press.

Bekker, C. J. (2009). Towards a theoretical model of Christian leadership. *Journal of Biblical Perspectives in Leadership, 2*(2), 142-152.

Berkhof, L. (1996). *Systematic theology.* Grand Rapids, MI: William B. Eerdman.

Blanchard, K., & Hodges, P. (2005). *Lead like Jesus: Lessons from the greatest leadership role model of all time.* Nashville, TN: Thomas Nelson.

Blum, E. A. (1981). *The expositor's Bible commentary: Volume 12.* Grand rapids, MI: Zondervan.

Bouyer, L. (1975). The priest and the eucharist. In R. E. Terwilliger & U. T. Holmes, III (Eds.), *To be a priest* (pp. 103-109). New York, NY: Seabury Press.

Breisach, E. (2007). *Historiography: Ancient, medieval, and modern* (3rd ed.). Chicago, IL: University of Chicago Press.

Burke, K. (1968). *Counter statement*. Los Angeles, CA: University of California Press.

Cameron, K. S., & Quinn, R. E. (2006). *Diagnosing and changing organizational culture*. San Francisco, CA: Jossey-Bass.

Campbell, B. L. (1998) *Honor, shame, and the rhetoric of 1 Peter*. Atlanta, GA: Scholars Press.

Canton, J. (2007). *The extreme future: The top ten trends that will reshape the world in the next 20 years*. New York, NY: Penguin.

Chan, A., Hannah, S., & Gardner, W. (2005). Veritable authentic leadership: Emergence, functioning and impacts. In W. Gardner & B. Avolio (Eds.), *Authentic leadership theory and practice: Origins, effects, and development* (pp. 3-42). San Diego, CA: Elsevier.

Ciulla, J. B. (2004). *Ethics: The heart of leadership*. Westport, CT: Greenwood.

Clinton, J. R. (1988). *The making of a leader*. Colorado Springs, CO: Navpress.

Clowney, E. (1988). *The message of 1 Peter*. Downers Grove, Il: InterVarsity Press.

Collins, J. (2001). *Good to great: Why some companies make the leap and others don't*. New York, NY: HarperCollins.

Collins, M. K. (2006). *The power of leadership: The heartbeat of God.* Hampton, VA: CFI.

Conner, K. J. (1989). *The church in the New Testament.* Chichester, England: Sovereign World.

Cooper, C., Scandura, T., & Schriesheim, C. (2005). Looking forward but learning from our past: Potential challenges to developing authentic leadership theory and authentic leaders. *The Leadership Quarterly, 16*(3), 475-494.

Creswell, J. (2009). *Research design: Qualitative, quantitative, and mixed methods approach.* Thousand Oaks, CA: Sage.

Crisp, O. (2007). *Divinity and humanity: The incarnation reconsidered.* New York, NY: Cambridge University Press.

Damazio, F. (1988). *The making of a leader.* Portland, OR: Bible Temple.

Danley, D. A. (2009). Toward an understanding of the kenosis of Christ: A proposed a priori constituent to transformative leadership traits in Philippians 2:5-11 (Doctoral dissertation). *Dissertation Abstracts International: Section A, 71*(11). (UMI No. 3425736)

Davids, P. H. (1990). *The first epistle of Peter: New international commentary on the New Testament.* Grand Rapids, MI: William B. Eerdmans.

Davis, D. B. (1975). *The problem of slavery in the age of revolution 1770-1823.* Ithaca, NY: Cornell University Press.

Day, D. V. (2000). Leadership development: A review in context. *The Leadership Quarterly, 11*(4), 581-613.

DeWeese, G. J., & Moreland, J. P. (2005). *Philosophy made slightly less difficult*. Downers Grove, IL: InterVarsity Press.

Donahue, J. R. (1994). Redaction criticism: Has the hauptstrasse become a sackgasse? In E. McKnight & E. Malbon (Eds.), *The new literary criticism and the New Testament* (pp. 27-57). Valley Forge, PA: Trinity Press.

Douglas, C., Ferris, G., & Perrewe, P. (2005). Leader political skill and authentic leadership. In W. Gardner & B. Avolio (Eds.), *Authentic leadership theory and practice: Origins, effects, and development* (pp. 139-144). San Diego, CA: Elsevier.

Eagly, A. (2005). Achieving relational authenticity in leadership: Does gender matter? *The Leadership Quarterly, 16*(3), 459-474.

Elliot, J. H. (1986). Social–scientific criticism of the New Testament and its social world. *Society of Biblical Literature (Semeia), 35,* 1-33.

Elliot, J. H. (1993). *What is social–scientific criticism?* Minneapolis, MN: Fortress Press.

Elliot, J. H. (2000). *The anchor Bible: I Peter.* New Haven CT: Yale University Press.

Elliot, J. H. (2007). *Conflict, community, and honor: 1 Peter in social–scientific perspective.* Eugene, OR: Wipf & Stock.

Esler, P. F. (1987). *Community and gospel in Luke-Acts: The social and political motivations of Lukan theology.* New York, NY: Cambridge University Press.

Farling, M. L., Stone, A. G., & Winston, B. E. (1999). Servant leadership: Setting the stage for empirical research. *The Journal of Leadership Studies, 6,* 49-72.

Faulhaber, J. (2007). The role of tribulation and virtue in

creativity: A sacred texture analysis of 1 Peter. *Journal of Biblical Perspectives in Leadership, 1*(2), 135-147.

Fee, G. (1995). *Paul's letter to the Philippians.* Grand Rapids, MI: William B. Eerdmans.

Fee, G., & Stuart, D. (1993). *How to read the Bible for all its worth: A guide to understanding the Bible.* Grand Rapids, MI: Zondervan.

Fiedler, F. (1967). *A theory of leadership effectiveness.* New York: McGraw-Hill.

Flick, U. (2002). *An introduction to qualitative research.* Thousand Oaks, CA: Sage.

Fowler, R. (1986). *Linguistic criticism.* Oxford, England: Oxford University Press.

Friberg, T., & Friberg, B. (2000). *Analytical lexicon to the Greek New Testament.* Grand Rapids, MI: Baker Book House.

Fry, L. (2003). Toward a theory of spiritual leadership. *Leadership Quarterly, 14*(6), 693-727.

Fry, L. (2005). In search of authenticity: Spiritual leadership theory as a source for future theory, research, and practice on authentic leadership. In W. Gardner & B. Avolio (Eds.), *Authentic leadership theory and practice: Origins, effects, and development* (pp. 183-202). San Diego, CA: Elsevier.

Galbraith, C. S., & Galbraith, O. (2004). *The Benedictine rule of leadership.* Avon, MA: Adams Media.

Gardner, W., & Avolio, B. (Eds.) (2005). *Authentic leadership theory and practice: Origins, effects, and development: Vol. 3. Monographs in leadership and management.* New York, NY: Elsevier Science.

Gardner, W., Avolio, B., Luthans, F., May, D., & Walumbwa, F. (2005). "Can you see the real me?" A self-based model of authentic leader and follower development. *The Leadership Quarterly, 16*(3), 343-372.

George, B. (2007). *True north: Discover your authentic leadership.* San Francisco, CA: Jossey-Bass.

Gibbons, S. (2008). Spiritual formation: The basis for all leading. *Inner Resources for Leaders, 1*, 1-9.

Gray, D. R. (2008). Christological hymn: The leadership paradox of Philippians 2:5-11. *Journal of Biblical Perspectives in Leadership, 2*(1), 3-18.

Greene, J. (2007). *1 Peter: Two horizons New Testament commentary.* Grand Rapids, MI: William B. Eerdmans.

Grudem, W. (1994). *Systematic theology: An introduction to biblical doctrine.* Grand Rapids, MI: Zondervan.

Grudem, W. (1999). *The first epistle of Peter: An introduction and commentary.* Grand Rapids, MI: William B. Eerdmans.

Guinness, O. (1993). *Dining with the Devil: The mega church movement flirts with modernity.* Grand Rapids, MI: Baker Book House

Guinness, O. (2000). *When no one sees: The importance of character in an age of image.* Colorado Springs, CO: Navpress.

Guinness, O. (2003). *The call: Finding and fulfilling the central purpose of your life.* Nashville, TN: W Publishing.

Hannah, S., Lester, P., & Vogelgesang, G. (2005). Moral leadership: Explicating the moral component of authentic leadership. In W. Gardner & B. Avolio (Eds.), *Authentic leadership theory and practice: Origins, effects, and development* (pp. 43-82). San Diego, CA: Elsevier.

Hardgrove, M. E. (2008). The Christ hymn as a song for leaders. *Journal of Biblical Perspectives in Leadership, 2*(1), 19-31.

Hart, T. (2000). Tradition, authority, and a Christian approach to the Bible as Scripture. In J. B. Green & M. Turner (Eds.), *Between two horizons: Spanning New Testament studies & systematic theology* (pp. 183-204). Grand Rapids, MI: Wm. B. Eerdmans.

Hawthorne, G. (1983). *Word Biblical commentary: Philippians.* Waco, TX: Word Books.

Herdt, J. A. (2008). *Putting on virtue: The legacy of the splendid vices.* Chicago, IL: University of Chicago Press.

Hiebert, D. (1992). *1 Peter.* Winona Lake, IN: BMH Books.

Hjalmarson, L. (2006). Theological reflections on leadership. Retrieved from http://nextreformation.com/wp-dmin/resources/reflections.pdf

House, R. J. (1971). A path–goal theory of leader effectiveness. *Administrative Science Quarterly, 16,* 321-328.

House, R. J., Hanges, P. J., Javidian, M., Dorfman, P. W., & Gupta, V. (2004). *Culture, leadership, and organizations: The GLOBE study of 62 societies.* Thousand Oaks, CA: Sage.

Hughes, L. (2005). Developing transparent relationships through humor in the authentic leader–follower relationship. In W. Gardner & B. Avolio (Eds.), *Authentic leadership theory and practice: Origins, effects, and development* (pp. 83-106). San Diego, CA: Elsevier.

Hughes, R. L., & Beatty, K. C. (2005). *Becoming a strategic leader: Your role in your organization's enduring success*. San Francisco, CA: Jossey-Bass.

Iles, R., Morgeson, F., & Nahrgang, J. (2005). Authentic leadership and eudaemonic well-being: *Leadership Quarterly, 16*(3), 373-394.

Jobes, K (2005). *1 Peter: Baker exegetical commentary on the New Testament*. Grand Rapids. MI: Baker Academic.

Kerlinger, F., & Lee, H. (2000). *Foundations of behavioral research*. Orlando, FL: Harcourt College.

Klenke, K. (2005). The internal theater of the authentic leader: Integrating cognitive, affective, and spiritual facets of authentic leadership. In W. Gardner & B. Avolio (Eds.), *Authentic leadership theory and practice: Origins, effects, and development* (pp. 155-182). San Diego, CA: Elsevier.

Klenke, K. (2007). Authentic leadership: A self, leader, and spiritual identity perspective. *International Journal of Leadership Studies, 3*(1), 68-97.

Kouzes, J., M., & Posner, B. Z. (2007). *The leadership challenge*. San Francisco, CA: Jossey-Bass.

Leahy, K. (2010). A study of Peter as a model of servant leadership. *Inner Resources for Leaders, 2*(4), 1-10.

Luthans, F., & Avolio, B. (2003). Authentic leadership: A positive development approach. In K. Cameron, J. Dutton, & R. Quinn (Eds.), *Positive organizational scholarship* (pp. 241-258). San Francisco: Berrett-Koehler.

Luther, M. (1990). *Commentary on Peter and Jude*. Grand Rapids, MI: Kregel.

Machiavelli, N. (1908). *The prince* (W. K. Marriott, Trans.). Retrieved from http://www.constitution.org/mac/prince.pdf (Original work published 1515)

Marshall, I. H. (1991). *1 Peter: IVP New Testament commentary*. Downers Grove, IL: InterVarsity Press.

Martin, R. P. (1997). *A hymn of Christ: Philippians 2:5-11 in recent interpretation and in the setting of early Christian worship*. Downers Grove, IL: InterVarsity Press.

Mcbrien, R. P. (2000). *Lives of the popes: The pontiffs from St. Peter to John Paul II*. San Francisco, CA: HarperCollins.

McClymond, M. J. (2001). Prophet or loss? Reassessing Max Weber's theory of religious leadership. In D. N. Freedman & M. J. McClymond (Eds.), *The rivers of paradise: Moses, Buddha, Confucius, Jesus and Muhammad as religious founders* (pp. 613-658). Grand Rapids: Wm. B. Eerdmans.

McGrath, A. E. (2002). *The future of Christianity*. Malden, MA: Blackwell.

McKnight, E., & Malbon, E. (1994). *The new literary criticism and the New Testament*. Valley Forge, PA: Trinity Press.

Michie, S., & Gooty, J. (2005). Values, emotions, and authenticity: Will the real leaders please stand up? *The Leadership Quarterly, 16,* 441-458.

Moreland, J. P., & Craig, W. L. (2003). *Philosophical foundations for a Christian worldview*. Downers Grove, IL: InterVarsity Press.

Morris, A. J., Brotheridge, C. M., & Urbanski, J. C. (2005). Bringing humility to leadership: Antecedents and consequences of leader humility. *Human Relations, 58*(10), 1323-1350.

Navone, J. (1989). *Self-giving and sharing: The Trinity and human fulfillment.* Collegeville, MN: Liturgical Press.

Niewold, J. W. (2006). Incarnational leadership: Towards a distinctly Christian theory of leadership (Doctoral dissertation). *Dissertation Abstracts International: Section A, 67*(11). (Publication No. AAT 3243512)

Norris, S. E. (2008). Authentic Christological leadership revealed through sacred texture analysis of the Philippians hymn (2:5-11). *Inner Resources for Leaders, 2,* 1-14.

Northouse, P. G. (2004). *Leadership: Theory and practice.* Thousand Oaks, CA: Sage.

O'Brien, P. (1991). *The epistle to the Philippians: A commentary on the Greek text.* Grand Rapids, MI: William B. Eerdmans.

Ong, W. J. (2002). *Orality and literacy:* New York, NY: Routledge, Toylor, and Francis.

Patterson, K. (2003). *Servant leadership: A theoretical model.* Paper presented at the Servant Leadership Research Roundtable, Virginia Beach, VA.

Patton, M. (2002). *Qualitative research and evaluation methods.* Thousand Oaks, CA: Sage.

Perelman, C. (1982). *The realm of rhetoric.* Notre Dame: The University of Notre Dame Press.

Perkins, P. (2000). *Peter: Apostle for the whole church.* Minneapolis, MN: Fortress Press.

Polkinghorne, J. (2007). *Quantum physics and theology: An unexpected kinship.* New Haven, CT: Yale University Press.

Powell, M. A. (1990). *What is narrative criticism?* Minneapolis, MN: Fortress Press.

Power, D. (1998). *A spiritual theology of the priesthood: The mystery of Christ and the mission of the priest.* Washington, DC: The Catholic University of America Press.

Reid, K. (2009). *Kenosis as a gift to humanity of God's grace to be lived relationally* (Unpublished Master's thesis, Melbourne College of Divinity). Retrieved from http://repository.mcd.edu.au/877/1/2011Th_MA(Theol)(MinorThesis)_ReidCK_Kenosis_as_a_Gift_to_Humanity_of_God's_Grace.pdf

Richard, M. E. (1897). *Philip Jacob Spener and his work.* Philadelphia, PA: Lutheran Publication Society.

Robbins, V. K. (1984). *Jesus the teacher: A socio-rhetorical interpretation of Mark.* Philadelphia, PA: Fortress Press.

Robbins, V. K. (1994). Socio-rhetorical criticism: Mary, Elizabeth, and the magnificat as a test case. In E. McKnight & E. Malbon (Eds.), *The new literary criticism and the New Testament* (pp. 164-209). Valley Forge, PA: Trinity Press.

Robbins, V. K. (1996). *Exploring the texture of texts: A guide to socio-rhetorical interpretation.* Harrisburg, PA: Trinity Press.

Robbins, V. K. (2004). *Beginnings and developments in socio-rhetorical interpretation.* Retrieved from http://www.religion.emory.edu/faculty/robbins/Pdfs/SRIBegDevRRA.pdf

Roberts, K. A. (1978). Toward a generic concept of counter-culture. *Sociological Focus,* (11), 111-126.

Rohman, C. (1999). *A world of ideas.* New York, NY: Ballantine Books.

Seagraves, D. (2010). *1 Peter: Standing fast in the grace of God.* Hazelwood, MO: Word Aflame Press.

Schaff, P. (1885). *Ante-Nicene fathers: The apostolic fathers with Justin Martyr and Ireneus:* Retrieved from http://www.ccel.org/ccel/schaff/anf01.pdf

Self, C. (2009). Love and organizational leadership: An intertexture analysis of 1 Corinthians 13 (Doctoral dissertation). *Dissertation Abstracts International: Section A, 70*(10). (UMI No. 337775)

Senge, P. M. (2006). *The art and practice of learning organizations.* New York, NY: Random House.

Shamir, B., & Eilam, G. (2005). "What's your story?" A life-stories approach to authentic leadership development. *The Leadership Quarterly, 16(3),* 395-418.

Sheldrake, P. (2007). *A brief history of spirituality: Blackwell brief histories of religion.* Malden, MA: Blackwell.

Sparrowe, R. (2005) Authentic leadership and the narrative self. *The Leadership Quarterly, 16,* 419-440.

Spencer, J. L. (2008). *Peter: A phenomenology of leadership.* Paper presented at Biblical Perspectives in Leadership Research Roundtable, Virginia Beach, VA.

Spener, P. J. (1964). *Pious desires* (T. G. Tappert, Trans.). Minneapolis, MN: Fortress Press. (Original work published 1675)

Turner, M. (2000). Historical criticism and theological hermeneutics of the New Testament. In J. B. Green & M. Turner (Eds.), *Between two horizons: Spanning New Testament studies & systematic theology* (pp. 183-204). Grand Rapids, MI: Wm. B. Eerdmans.

Turner, M., & Green, J. (2000). New Testament commentary and systematic theology: Strangers or friends. In J. B. Green & M. Turner (Eds.), *Between two horizons: Spanning New Testament studies & systematic theology* (pp.1-22). Grand Rapids, MI: Wm. B. Eerdmans.

Webb, E. (2009). *Worldview and mind: Religious thought and psychological development.* Columbia, MI: The University of Missouri Press.

Weber, M. (1968). *Economy and society* (G. Roth & C. Wittich, Trans.). New York, NY: Bedminster Press. (Original work published 1956)

Wheatley, M. (1999). *Leadership and the new science: Discovering order in a chaotic world.* San Francisco, CA: Berrett-Koehler.

Willard, D. (1997). *The divine conspiracy: Rediscovering our hidden life in God.* New York, NY: HarperCollins.

Wilson, B. R. (1969). A typology of sects. In R. Robertson (Ed.), *Sociology of religion* (pp. 361-383). Baltimore, MD: Penguin.

Winston, B. (2002). *Be a leader for God's sake.* Virginia Beach, VA: School of Global Leadership and Entrepreneurship.

Wire, A. (1994). Since God is one: Rhetoric as theology and history in Paul's Romans. In E. McKnight & E. Malbon

(Eds.), *The new literary criticism and the New Testament* (pp. 210-227). Valley Forge, PA: Trinity Press.

Witherington, B. (2007). *Letter and homilies for Hellenized Christians: A socio-rhetorical commentary on 1-2 Peter.* Downers Grove, IL: InterVarsity Press.

Witherington, B. (2009a). *The indelible image: The theological and ethical thought of the New Testament* (Vol. 1). Downers Grove, IL: InterVarsity Press.

Witherington, B. (2009b). *What's in the word: Rethinking the socio-rhetorical character of the New Testament.* Waco, TX: Baylor University Press.

Wortham, R. A. (1996). Christology a community identity in the Philippians hymn: The Philippians hymn as social drama (Philippians 2:5-11). *Perspectives in Religious Studies, 23*(3), 269-287.

Wright, N. T. (1992). *The climax of the covenant: Christ and the law in Pauline theology.* Minneapolis, MN: First Fortress Press.

Wuest, K. S. (1966). *Wuest's word studies: Philippians in the Greek New Testament for the English reader.* Grand Rapids, MI: Wm. B. Eerdman.

Youssef, C., & Luthans, F. (2005). Multi-level theory building for sustained performance. In W. Gardner & B. Avolio (Eds.), *Authentic leadership theory and practice: Origins, effects, and development* (pp. 303-344). San Diego, CA: Elsevier.

Yukl, G. (2002). *Leadership in organizations* (5th ed.). Upper Saddle River, NJ: Prentice-Hall.

Zarate, M. (2009). The leadership approach of Jesus in Matthew 4 and 5 (Doctoral dissertation). *Dissertation Abstracts International: Section A, 70*(10). (UMI No. 3377777)

Zook, T. D. (1993). An examination of leadership practices in large, Protestant congregations (Doctoral dissertation). *Dissertation Abstracts International: Section A, 54*(3), 968. (UMI No. 9318326).

ABOUT THE AUTHOR

Steven Crowther is president of Grace College of Divinity in Fayetteville, North Carolina, and directs leadership training centers in Venezuela and Brazil. Crowther holds a Master's degree in Theological Studies from Asbury Theological Seminary and a Ph.D. in Organizational Leadership with a major in Global Leadership from Regent University's School of Global Leadership & Entrepreneurship. In addition, he has been involved in pastoral ministry for over twenty years in various capacities, including associate and senior pastor roles.

www.ingramcontent.com/pod-product-compliance
Lightning Source LLC
Chambersburg PA
CBHW060519100426
42743CB00009B/1380